Effective Time Management

Susan Herman

Effective Time Management

Part Number: 088606
Course Edition: 1.0

Acknowledgments

Project Team

Content Developer: Susan Herman • **Content Manager:** Clare Dygert • **Graphic Designer:** Tracie Drake • **Project Coordinator:** Gail Henry • **Content Editor:** Laura Telford • **Materials Editor:** Elizabeth Fuller • **Business Matter Expert:** Sharon Melville • **Project Technical Support:** Mike Toscano

NOTICES

EFFECTIVE TIME MANAGEMENT

CONTENTS

LESSON 5: CREATING AN ACTION PLAN

NOTES

ABOUT THIS COURSE

Time is a form of currency, and the ways that we talk about it illustrate its value: we say "Time is money," and "My time was well spent," or "It's a waste of time." Like most professionals, you've probably struggled with managing this resource effectively. In this course, you will practice techniques that will help you achieve more effective use of your time so that you can direct your energy towards the activities that will further your professional and personal goals.

Your time is a precious and finite resource. Too often, you may feel frustrated that there aren't enough hours in the day to accomplish everything you hope to do. Effective time managers enjoy the satisfaction of directing their talents and energy towards productive, goal-centered activities. By identifying improved time management and organizational skills, you, too, can utilize your time and energy effectively, focusing your efforts on the activities that will help you reach your goals.

Course Description

Target Student

Professionals in a variety of fields who are seeking improved time-management skills so that they can perform more effectively.

Course Prerequisites

There are no prerequisites for this course.

How to Use This Book

As a Learning Guide

Each lesson covers one broad topic or set of related topics. Lessons are arranged in order of increasing proficiency; skills you acquire in one lesson are used and developed in subsequent lessons. For this reason, you should work through the lessons in sequence.

We organized each lesson into results-oriented topics. Topics include all the relevant and supporting information you need to master the material, and activities allow you to apply this information to practical hands-on examples.

All Element K soft skills courses offer business simulations. These business simulations immerse you in a comfortable environment where you are presented with situations that require you to make real world decisions based on the principles you have learned in the course. Within these simulations, you will meet characters, have access to clear and timely feedback, and have the ability to review and change previous decisions. These business simulations are available on the course CD-ROM and can be accessed from any computer having the software and hardware requirements specified in the Course Requirement section of your manual.

You get to try out each new skill on a specially prepared sample file. This saves you typing time and allows you to concentrate on the skill at hand. Through the use of sample files, hands-on activities, illustrations that give you feedback at crucial steps, and supporting background information, this book provides you with the foundation and structure to learn time-management skills quickly and easily.

As a Review Tool

Any method of instruction is only as effective as the time and effort you are willing to invest in it. In addition, some of the information that you learn in class may not be important to you immediately, but it may become important later on. For this reason, we encourage you to spend some time reviewing the topics and activities after the course. For additional challenge when reviewing activities, try the "What You Do" column before looking at the "How You Do It" column.

As a Reference

The organization and layout of the book make it easy to use as a learning tool and as an after-class reference. You can use this book as a first source for definitions of terms, background information on given topics, and summaries of procedures.

Course Objectives

In this course, you will identify effective time-management strategies, including defining personal and professional goals, establishing priorities, and identifying the tasks that will be critical to achieving those goals. You will create a personal time-management action plan.

You will:

- articulate your goals.

- analyze how you are currently allocating your most precious resources: energy and time.

- identify elements of your personal work style that contribute to your effective use of time.

- assemble a collection of time-management tools and strategies that you can use to take control of your time.

- create an action plan for your time-management process and identify ways to evaluate and improve your efforts.

Course Requirements

Hardware

- A Pentium 90MHz or better, or Macintosh PowerPC
- Screen resolution of 800 x 600 @ 256 colors

Software

- Operating Systems MS-Windows 95, 98, 2000, ME, NT 4.0, XP Home Edition, or XP Professional 2000.
- Microsoft Internet Explorer 5.0x, 5.5, 6.0; or Netscape Navigator (excluding 6.0 & 6.1)
- Adobe Acrobat Reader 6.0 or higher; Apple QuickTime 5.0 or higher; Macromedia Flash Player 6.0.79 or higher; or Macromedia Shockwave 7.0.2, 8.0, 8.5, 8.5.1 or higher
- Turn off pop-up blocking. (Internet Explorer Users only)

Class Setup

1. If you plan to use the overheads provided on the CD-ROM, set up an instructor computer.
2. If you plan to have students key the lesson level business simulations, set up a computer for each student participating in the class.

NOTES

Lesson 1
Defining Goals

Lesson Objectives:

In this lesson, you will articulate your goals.

You will:

- Define time management.
- Describe your big and small dreams, as well as your personal and professional dreams.
- Describe your big and small regrets, as well as your personal and professional regrets.
- Articulate your goals.

Introduction

People who are effective time managers are able to focus their efforts on achieving their long-term goals. Defining your goals is the first step towards managing your time effectively. You need to define your goals so that you know what you want to accomplish through improved time management. In this lesson, you will identify the basic underlying philosophy and processes of time management, and you will clearly articulate your goals for the future by identifying two critical guiding lights: your dreams and your regrets.

Like most professionals, you have probably struggled to accomplish everything on your daily to-do list. At the same time, you may find it difficult to focus on the things that are really important to your life, such as your dreams and goals for future successes. By implementing effective time management techniques, you will be better able to succeed both in your everyday routine and in your pursuit of long-term goals.

TOPIC A

Define Time Management

Before you can begin to reap the benefits of using your time more effectively, you must define what time management is. In this topic, you will define time management.

If you have struggled with effectively managing your time in the past, you may not realize that there is a process and a philosophy of time management that you can master and use to your great benefit. Defining time management will allow you to focus clearly on the processes involved.

Time Management Process

Time management is a strategic process for purposefully reallocating your finite resources and time to address goal-centered activities. The time management process doesn't require you to work longer hours or to keep endless to-do lists. But it will help you to structure your life with purpose, so that you can more effectively devote your energy to targeting your goals.

Table 1-1: *The Steps in the Process of Time Management*

Time Management Process	Actions
Step 1	Define the dreams that you hope to achieve and the regrets you have about accomplishments you have not made.
Step 2	Articulate the goals that you want to establish for yourself.
Step 3	Analyze your current allocation of energy.
Step 4	Identify how you are currently using your time.
Step 5	Analyze your current tasks and daily workload.
Step 6	Identify how you like to work.
Step 7	Identify your personal strengths.
Step 8	Reduce the influences that steal time from you.

Time Management Process	Actions
Step 9	Assemble your time management tools, choosing tools that work for you.
Step 10	Create an action plan for time management.

ACTIVITY 1-1

Considering Time Management

Scenario:

Leah is a cookbook author; she supports her family with her book contracts while working out of her home office. Her husband, Tom, is a stay-at-home father to their two young children. Leah's work space doubles as the children's playroom, and is noisy, crowded, and chaotic. Tom often has trouble keeping the children entertained, and much of Leah's workday includes helping to care for the children. She rarely has an uninterrupted hour. Leah often finds herself staying up late at night to finish the day's work, while at the same time completing any household chores that weren't done during the day.

1. **Leah knows that she needs to improve her use of time. What is the first step for Leah?**

    a) Defining what it is that she hopes to accomplish.

    b) Identifying how she likes to work.

    c) Identifying her personal strengths.

    d) Creating an action plan for time management.

2. **Leah must be a competent person, since she has managed to become a published cookbook author. Why should she waste more time on time management, when she could just spend her time working harder?**

    a) Leah is already working hard, but she is not necessarily working effectively.

    b) Leah is not a competent person, as evidenced by her failure to get her work done each day.

    c) Leah's time-management problems would be solved if she had an office outside of her home.

    d) Leah has the same problem that many working mothers have, and there is no solution until the children are grown.

ACTIVITY 1-2

Defining Time Management

Scenario:

As you reflect on the following questions, consider their relevance to your efforts to improve your time management skills.

1. What do you think of the time-management process as it was defined? How does this change or influence your understanding of time management?

2. How do you anticipate that your time-management process will be influenced by thinking about your dreams for the future? In what ways do you think this will guide your efforts?

3. What are some of the everyday problems that you have with your time management? What are some of the things you hope to do differently as a result of working through this process?

TOPIC B

Describe Your Dreams

Your dreams are the guiding lights for your life. By describing your dreams, both big and small, both personal and professional, you can begin to think strategically about what you hope to accomplish in life. The choices you make about spending time today will influence the feasibility of attaining your dreams tomorrow. In this topic, you will define what constitutes a dream and then describe your dreams.

People who are able to consistently set new goals and achieve them have mastered the ability to focus their energies on the things that are important to them. By describing your dreams, you can begin to focus your thinking strategically and focus your energy on the activities that will further your efforts.

Dreams

Definition:

A *dream* is your personal vision for yourself; it embodies the hopes that you have for your future achievements. Your dreams are very personal and they are unique to you. They may encompass your ideas about your career development, educational advancement, or other milestones. Dreams come in different forms. They may relate to your professional or personal life. They may be grand and ambitious or quite small.

Example:

Jack, an accountant, can envision several dreams for his future. He wants to advance his career by achieving a better position with more responsibility and a higher salary. He has had a lifelong dream of overcoming his fear of public speaking. On a personal level, he dreams of making friends and having a more active social life.

Non-Example:

Daydreams are flights of fancy; they focus on events that are beyond your control. Thinking about winning the lottery is a daydream. Because it is an unrealistic fantasy, it is not relevant to the process of improving your time-management skills.

Dreams

Although it is a valuable exercise, some people find it difficult to devote time to considering their dreams. The more effort you invest in this part of the process, the more valuable you may ultimately find this course.

How to Describe Your Dreams

A good description of your dreams includes a succinct, clear vision for a big dream, a small dream, a personal dream, and a professional dream.

Guidelines

To describe your dreams, follow these guidelines:

- Consider the grand or ambitious achievements you'd like to make:
    — Consider the achievements you'd like to make that would benefit your family.
    — Consider the long-term financial achievements you'd like to make.
    — Consider the milestones you'd like to reach in your career.
    — If you have trouble envisioning a big dream that is within the realm of possibility, begin by finishing this sentence: "If I could find the time, I would ___."
- Consider the small improvements or changes you'd like to realize:
    — Consider any habits you would like to change.
    — Consider the small steps you could take towards big dreams.
    — If you have trouble envisioning your life differently than it is now, begin by identifying one small dream. Reflect on yesterday. Note one thing that you wish you had been able to accomplish yesterday. Use that reflection as the basis for a small dream.
- Identify what you'd like to improve or develop in your personal life.

- Identify what you hope to achieve professionally in your current job path, career, or education.
- Make sure that the dreams you have identified are possible and within your control:
  - If the dreams you have identified are unrealistic flights of fancy, set those aside. Focus on other dreams that are within the realm of possibility.
- Describe your dreams in one to four sentences.

Example:

Michael, a divorced father of two, is a financial planner working for a large multinational corporation. He has trouble juggling all of the activities he wants to incorporate into his schedule. He has described his dreams; his big dream is to retire at 55, and his small dream is to spend more time each day with his children.

His personal dream is to run the Boston Marathon. His professional dream is to attain a management position within his firm. Michael believes these dreams are possible and within his control.

DISCOVERY ACTIVITY 1-3

Describing Dreams

Scenario:

Deborah has been working as a special education teacher in a large school district for more than a decade. She has job security, but feels bored by the routine and sees no clear path for advancement. She wants to increase her earning potential and take on new challenges, but she doesn't know how to make a transition. Meanwhile, she rarely has time for her favorite creative pursuits, such as painting and gardening. She works from early morning until evening every day, and finds herself frequently exhausted by her emotionally demanding job. She has only vague ideas about how to effect changes in her future.

1. **If Deborah is having trouble getting started, how should she begin describing her dreams?**

    a) She should make a comprehensive list of everything she wants to do.

    b) She should postpone describing her dreams until she finds some free time.

    c) She should focus on the obstacles standing in her way.

    d) She should identify one small dream.

2. Ideally, the dreams that Deborah identifies should have certain characteristics. Which of these are among them?

    a) Deborah's dreams should relate to what she hopes her employer will offer her.

    b) Deborah's dreams should be fantastic and "pie in the sky."

    c) Deborah's dreams can be large or small as long as they are within the realm of possibility.

    d) Deborah should identify what she'd like to improve or develop in her personal life.

DISCOVERY ACTIVITY 1-4

Discussing Dreams

Scenario:

Reflect on your dreams, and use your own experiences and ideas to contribute to the group discussion.

1. What are some of the big achievements you'd like to make? How do you think it would benefit you or your family if you achieved them? What are some of the milestones you'd like to reach in your career?

2. What are some of the small improvements you'd like to make? What are some habits you think you might like to change? Are there any small dreams that you think you could achieve within the next six months?

3. Have you ever considered time-management within the context of dreams before? How do you think reflecting on your dreams for the future will influence your efforts to manage your time?

4. Once you've given some thought to focusing on your dreams, do you think this will change how you think about using time as a resource? Why or why not? Do you think that keeping your mind on what you hope to accomplish over the long term can help you use your time well today?

5.   Is this the first time in your professional life that you've thought carefully about your dreams for the future? Do you find it easy or difficult to think about time management within the context of long-term planning? Are you a person who enjoys planning for the future, or do you prefer to focus on today?

TOPIC C

Identify Regrets

Our dreams tell us where we'd like to go in life. Our regrets about the past are valuable teaching tools, too. By identifying your regrets, you can make better, more informed choices for yourself in the future. Now that you have described your dreams, you will identify your regrets. In this topic, you will describe your regrets.

Identifying your regrets will help you to think more strategically about your future because it will help you to pinpoint the areas in which you want to improve. Identifying your regrets will help you to avoid repeating similar mistakes in the future. Identifying past mistakes related to wasted time and missed opportunities will also help you to make tactical decisions about improving your use of time.

Regrets

Definition:

A *regret* is the disappointment you experience due to missed opportunities or unfulfilled potential. A regret is a personal, privately held sense of failure. In the context of time management, regrets relate to choices and events that are within your control or relate to your perception of your own shortcomings. You may have regrets that relate to any or all parts of life: your career, your educational achievements, or your personal life.

Example:

Polly was a state track champion in college. She hasn't found time to run in at least five years. She regrets that she did not pursue an advanced degree when she had the chance. She also feels guilty that she rarely finds enough time for her friends and family.

How to Identify Regrets

A good description of your regrets includes a clear articulation of a big regret, a small regret, a personal regret, and a professional regret.

Guidelines

To describe your regrets, follow these guidelines:

*   Identify something that is important to you that you wish you had done, or not done, or a choice that you made that had repercussions on your life.

- Identify something that causes you minor annoyance and disappointment. It may not have huge repercussions for your quality of life, but you wish you had acted differently.

- Identify something that bothers you personally because you have done something negative, or failed to do something positive. It may not affect anyone other than yourself.

- Identify something that you wish you had done, or not done, in your professional life.
  — Make sure that the regret relates to a choice that was within your control.
  — If you are having difficulty thinking of a relevant regret, complete this sentence: "I wish that five years ago, I had _____."

- Be specific, and describe your regrets in one to four sentences.

Example:

Marcus, a sales executive, has spent time making a list of his regrets. When Marcus was younger, he was less focused on longer range goals. As a result, he never finished college. "My big regret is that I wish that I had finished my bachelor's degree."

Thinking about choices he made earlier in life also leads Marcus to think about his finances. "My personal regret is that I wish I hadn't blown so much money when I was younger."

Marcus has been a hard worker and dedicated a lot of time to being successful at his career. But this has had a downside. "My small regret is that I don't have a wider circle of friends."

And although he has been very successful as a sales executive, Marcus hasn't pushed himself to the next level. "My professional regret is that I've always privately thought I could be a great sales manager, but I haven't had the confidence to pursue management jobs." Marcus has described his regrets in four sentences.

DISCOVERY ACTIVITY 1-5

Describing Your Regrets

Scenario:

Jackson is a busy realtor with teenaged twin daughters. He works long hours, including most evenings and weekends. He devotes any free time that he has to helping his daughters with their homework and attending their lacrosse and field hockey games. Jackson is satisfied with his life, except that he is frequently late for appointments, never has time to eat properly, and always feels the pressure of being up against a deadline. He's always pressed for time and can't figure out why there never seem to be enough hours in the day.

1. **Jackson wants to describe his regrets. What should he consider?**

   a) He should consider past events that were beyond his control.

   b) He should consider past events that had little bearing on his life.

   c) He should consider the regrets of other people around him.

   d) He should consider choices he's made that have had repercussions for his life.

2. **Jackson has many regrets. Which of the following are among the regrets that Jackson should consider relevant for the purposes of improving his time management?**

   a) Jackson's professional regret is that he doesn't have the MBA that would help him pursue management positions.

   b) Jackson's big regret is that he allowed himself to run up significant debt many years ago.

   c) Jackson's personal regret is that he never had the son he always wanted.

   d) Jackson's small regret is that he never keeps his New Year's resolution to lose 10 pounds.

DISCOVERY ACTIVITY 1-6

Discussing Regrets

Scenario:

Consider your regrets, and insofar as you are comfortable sharing them, use your ideas to contribute to the group discussion.

1. What is something that you wish you had done, or not done, in your professional life in the past? How has this awareness of a past professional regret informed the choices that you make on the job now?

2. Is there a regret that you identified that causes you minor annoyance and irritation? How will the awareness of this minor regret change or influence your behavior moving forward?

3. What do you think about using your regrets about the past as part of the basis for thinking about using time effectively? Do you think this will be helpful to you? Why or why not?

4. In this topic, we reviewed guidelines for identifying regrets. What did you discover about your regrets as a result of this process? Were there any surprises for you?

5. In your professional life, have you given thought to regrets before, or are you more focused on the future? How do you think it might help you to manage your time better if you think about your regrets? What part of this topic did you find most helpful as you think about making better time-management choices?

TOPIC D

Articulate Goals

You want to articulate your goals so that you know what you want to accomplish in the short-term and in the long-term. By articulating your goals, you will gain a clear vision of where you hope to be headed. In this topic, you will articulate your goals.

It's difficult to strive for and achieve new goals when all of your current resources of time and energy are being consumed ineffectively. By articulating your goals, you will be in a better position to make strategic choices about where to spend your energy and time. Articulating your goals will give you a clear vision of what you hope to achieve, both in the short-term and in the long-term, so that you can begin to align your energy and time with goal-centered activities.

Well-articulated Goals

Definition:

A *goal* is an end; it is an achievement or accomplishment that you are determined to reach in the future. A goal is more structured than a hope or a dream; it requires making plans and structuring your behavior accordingly. A well articulated goal is a clear, specific description of your expectations about the achievements or accomplishments you want to reach. It includes a time frame for completion.

Example:

Sandra, a public relations assistant, made a list of goals related to her professional life and her time management. She knew that her goals included the achievements she's determined to reach and that they're more structured than a hope. Her short-term goal is to sign up for one business management course; her long-term goal is to complete her business degree. Sandra's description is clear and specific, and she included a time frame.

Long-term and Short-term Goals

For the purposes of time management, long-term goals are goals that you hope to accomplish over a period of five years. Short-term goals are goals that you hope to accomplish within a shorter window of time that you define, such as two weeks, two months, or a year.

How to Articulate Goals

A good description of your goals clearly outlines what you expect of yourself.

Guidelines

To articulate your goals, follow these guidelines:

- Include a time frame for completion.
- Be as specific as you can in describing the behavior you expect of yourself.
- Review your descriptions of your dreams. Consider your dreams, and determine which of these will become the basis for your goals.

- Consider your descriptions of your regrets. Use the information you compiled here to shape your goals for the future.

- Write one sentence that describes a goal you expect to reach in the coming weeks or months.

- Write one sentence that describes a goal you expect to reach in the coming years.

- If you are having difficulty articulating your goals, begin by completing these sentences:
  — "In the next two weeks, I really want to complete _____."
  — "I would feel a great sense of accomplishment if I could accomplish _____."
  — "By this time next year, I want to be _____."

- Make sure that your goals are challenging but achievable. You want to set goals that require you to grow and change, but they should be within the bounds of what you can feasibly accomplish.

- Describe your goals in one or two sentences.

Example: Articulating Goals

Reginald is a stay-at-home father of three hoping to develop a career path. He starts by reviewing his dreams. Reginald has always wanted to work in a field where he can help others. He has always felt that he would like to be a member of a healthcare profession. Next, Reginald examines his regrets. He realizes that he wants a viable career and he regrets not pursuing an education.

As he considers his goals, he includes a time frame and specific expectations for himself.

His short-term goal is to complete the paperwork to enroll in courses to become a licensed practical nurse. His long-term goal is that by this time next year, he will be halfway through a two-year nursing program.

DISCOVERY ACTIVITY 1-7

Establishing Goals

Scenario:

C.J. is the manager of a customer service department and supervises four people. She prides herself on being a great mentor to the younger employees in her department, and she is available in her office more than 60 hours per week. Although she is well-liked and considered good at her job, C.J. frequently feels out of control and inefficient. She double-books her calendar, misses meetings, arrives late for appointments, and brings work home every weekend. Every day is filled with distractions and constant interruptions, making it very difficult for her to do any strategic planning for her career or her life.

1. C.J. has defined her goals this way: "I always wanted to be a nurse. I would like to go back to school someday for some kind of nursing job." Is this a good description of C.J.'s goals?

    a) No, because she has not investigated whether there are nursing jobs available in her area.

    b) Yes, this is an excellent description of C.J.'s goals.

    c) No, because C.J. has not included a proposed timeline or specific behavior that she expects of herself.

    d) No, because a good description of goals includes what she hopes other people will do for her.

2. C.J. needs to know whether she has appropriately described her goals. Which of the following accurately reflects a well-articulated goal?

    a) A good description of your goals clearly outlines what you expect of yourself.

    b) A well-articulated goal is a private hope that you probably will never achieve.

    c) A well-articulated goal implies that you know exactly how you will achieve it.

    d) A well-articulated goal is the same thing as a dream.

3. Why should C.J. spend time articulating her goals, when she can't even get her daily schedule under control?

    a) Articulating her goals will help C.J. strategize her time and energy allocation.

    b) C.J. will feel better about herself if she articulates her goals.

    c) C.J. needs to articulate her goals before she can choose a new, less stressful job or career path.

    d) Articulating her goals will give C.J. a welcome break from her office routine.

DISCOVERY ACTIVITY 1-8

Discussing Goals

Scenario:

Reflect on your goals, and use your ideas about goals to contribute to the group discussion.

1. Which dreams and regrets did you use as the basis for forming your goals? Can you describe one of the goals you have established for yourself?

2. Your goals should be challenging but achievable. What are some of the elements of your goals that will make them challenging for you? What factors have led you to conclude that your goals are also achievable?

3. Have you given much thought to your goals in the past? How effective have you been in meeting some of your goals?

4. Do you see any connection between your goals and how you choose to use your time today? How do you think your goals will influence how you use your time? Have you struggled with achieving goals in the past? How important do you think time management is in terms of pursuing your goals?

5. Do you think it's challenging to focus on goals for the future when each daily routine is perhaps very full? How do you think that focusing on your goals might change the way you approach each day?

Lesson 1 Follow-up

In this lesson, you described your dreams, identified your regrets, and articulated your goals.

1. Consider the importance of reflecting on your dreams and regrets. How do you anticipate using this information to your benefit as you approach the process of time management?

2. Reflect on the need to clearly articulate your own goals. What new insights did you glean about yourself and what you want to accomplish?

NOTES

LESSON 2

Analyzing Energy Allocation

Lesson Objectives:

In this lesson, you will analyze how you are currently allocating your most precious resources: energy and time.

You will:

*   Create a time log.

*   Analyze your current tasks.

*   Analyze your time usage.

*   Analyze your energy flow.

LESSON 2

Introduction

Effective time managers make informed, conscious choices about using their time and energy in the most effective manner possible. Analyzing your energy allocation is the first step towards making better choices. In this lesson, you will identify how your energy is spent, and then analyze your tasks, time usage, and energy flow.

In order to make sure that your precious resources aren't being wasted, you need to budget them. If you needed to budget your money, you would begin by determining where your funds are being spent currently. The same is true for budgeting your time and energy. You want to determine how you are currently spending your time and energy so that you can make better choices about spending these precious resources effectively.

TOPIC A

Identify How Energy Is Spent

In order to allocate your energy more strategically in the future, you must first identify how your energy is being spent currently. Where is most of your energy going? Your perception of your own energy expenditure may be different from the reality. In this topic, you will identify how your energy is being spent.

People who lack great time-management skills often don't realize how their energy is being frittered away. They may feel that they're working hard, but they don't experience an appropriate sense of satisfaction for their efforts. The benefit of identifying how your energy is being spent is that you will pinpoint how you are currently directing, or misdirecting, your energy.

Energy Allocation

Definition:

Energy allocation is the distribution of a person's energy, or effort, across activities. By analyzing your energy allocation, you can identify the activities that are consuming your energy.

Example:

David, a purchasing agent, complains that he can't complete his assignments within a regular 40-hour week. His supervisor, Marvin, has asked David to analyze his energy allocation so that they can identify the activities that are consuming David's energy and time.

Time Logs

Definition:

A *time log* is a written summary kept for a given period of time. It itemizes all of the activities completed during that time, and tracks the time allocated to each activity.

Example:

Allison has kept a time log for one 24-hour period. She tracked every activity during that period, writing down all of her activities and the length of time devoted to each. Allison noted even small tasks, such as phone calls, interruptions, and email.

TIME LOG

TIME	ACTIVITY
8:30am	Arrived at the office Check email Coffee break Visit with teammates
8:45am	Prepare materials for meeting
8:47am	Client phone call
9:00am	Meeting with clients
10:20am	Return phone calls, check email
10:35am	Review outstanding proposals on desk
10:41am	Client phone call
10:50am	Help John with sales questions
11:07am	Interrupted by Dave
11:15am	Prepare materials for sales conference
11:45am	Travel to client lunch
12:00pm	Lunch with clients
1:15pm	Return to office Check email
1:30pm	Meeting with supervisor

Figure 2-1: *A sample time log.*

Perception vs. Reality

Perception is an individual's mental concept of how time is spent. It exists in your mind. It may differ from the reality.

Reality is the totality of authentic things and events, or an objective assessment of effort and activities for a given period of time. It refers to how you actually spend your time and energy.

How to Create a Time Log

Procedure Reference: Create a Time Log

To create a time log, follow these guidelines.

1. Make sure you have pen, paper, and a clock available.

2. Determine how many hours you want to track through a time log. It should be at least three hours. A longer time log will yield more helpful data.

3. At the top of your time log, write "Time Log."

4. On the left side of the paper, mark regular intervals, such as "9:00," "10:00," and so on.

5. At the first hour mark, note the time and the activities you are doing at this time. Be as specific and detailed as possible.

6. Note all of your activities on your time log, including any diversions and interruptions.

7. Review the time log periodically to make sure you are not forgetting any activities.

8. Draw a star next to instances of productivity, in which you used your time effectively.

9. Draw a check mark next to instances of interruptions, distractions, and missed opportunities.

10. At the end of your time log, you should be able to summarize how much energy you have devoted to each activity or type of activity.

DISCOVERY ACTIVITY 2-1

Creating a Time Log

Scenario:

Roger owns a sporting goods store. His responsibilities include accounting, supervising employees, tracking inventory, ordering stock, and supervising the sales floor. Roger consistently feels overworked and pressured to compete with larger stores. He works hard every day, but his invoices are a chaotic mess, he's three days behind in returning phone calls, and he can't seem to get control of his paperwork or his schedule.

1. **Roger is keeping a time log in his office. At the end of the day today, he plans to jot down all of the activities he remembers. Which of the following is an accurate statement about Roger's time log?**

    a) Roger is completing the time log in accordance with the instructions.

    b) Roger needs to work on and revise the time log throughout the day.

    c) Roger won't benefit from keeping a time log until he gets his schedule under control.

    d) Roger should complete his time log on his day off, when he has free time.

2. **Which of the following statements about Roger's time log is true?**

    a) To save time, Roger can take good mental notes about his activities and fill in his time log later.

    b) Roger should include distractions and interruptions on his time log.

    c) Roger should only include productive activities on his time log.

    d) Roger should only include work-related activities on his time log.

3. **True or False? Roger should draw a check mark on his time log to highlight periods of productivity.**

    __ True

    __ False

DISCOVERY ACTIVITY 2-2

Discussing Time Logs

Scenario:

As you reflect on time logs, consider the questions below and share your ideas during the group discussion.

TIME LOG

TIME	ACTIVITY
8:30am	Arrived at the office Check email Coffee break Visit with teammates
8:45am	Prepare materials for meeting
8:47am	Client phone call
9:00am	Meeting with clients
10:20am	Return phone calls, check email
10:35am	Review outstanding proposals on desk
10:41am	Client phone call
10:50am	Help John with sales questions
11:07am	Interrupted by Dave
11:15am	Prepare materials for sales conference
11:45am	Travel to client lunch
12:00pm	Lunch with clients
1:15pm	Return to office Check email
1:30pm	Meeting with supervisor

Figure 2-2: *A sample time log.*

1. How do you think you might benefit from keeping a time log? Have you ever tried to track your time in the past? How do you think this exercise will influence your use of time?

2. Note the sample time log shown. How closely does this time log follow the recommended guidelines? Does the sample time log in any way fail to follow the recommended guidelines? How effective do you think this sample time log will be to the person who completed it? How could this person improve the time log? Please explain.

TOPIC B

Analyze Tasks

By analyzing the tasks that currently absorb your time and energy, you will be in a better position to make critical choices about time and energy allocation. In this topic, you will analyze tasks.

In the same way that you analyze your most important expenditures for a budget and then allocate the lion's share of your money to the most important expense items, you want to analyze your tasks and allocate the greatest amount of your time and energy to the most important. Analyzing your tasks will allow you to figure out exactly how you are spending your time and energy, leading you to a fuller understanding of how effectively you are leveraging these two precious resources.

Types of Tasks

There are different types of tasks. Tasks may be personal, professional, or recreational. Some tasks are assigned to you by others, while some tasks you've chosen for yourself. Some of your tasks are enjoyable.

DISCOVERY ACTIVITY 2-3

Analyzing Types of Tasks

Scenario:
Consider the following questions regarding types of activities.

1. **What are some of your personal tasks? What are some of your professional tasks? What are some of your recreational tasks?**

2. **Which of your tasks have been assigned to you by others? Which of your tasks have you chosen for yourself? Which of your tasks do you find enjoyable?**

Valuable Tasks

Definition:

A *valuable task* is a task that contributes to furthering your goals. A task that is valuable does not necessarily produce monetary gain. You may identify a task as valuable even if others do not consider it so.

Example:

Sara's long-term goal is to learn Spanish. Reading a daily Spanish-language newspaper is a valuable task for Sara because it will further her stated goal.

Critical Tasks

Definition:

A *critical task* is a task that must be completed. There are penalties for failing to complete critical tasks. Critical tasks may be job-related or personal. They may be assigned to you by others.

Example:

John is a reporter at a regional newspaper. He defined his critical tasks as writing the articles assigned to him by his editor, meeting his deadlines, and double-checking his facts. If John failed to perform any of these critical tasks, the penalty would be losing his job.

The 80/20 Rule

Management expert Joseph M. Juran developed a theory called the *80/20 rule*. It suggests that in any enterprise, 80 percent of the effort expended is nonessential, and 20 percent is essential. You can use the 80/20 rule to improve your effectiveness by focusing on the essential 20 percent of your tasks.

Origins of the 80/20 Rule

The 80/20 rule is sometimes incorrectly credited to the economist Vilfredo Pareto, who made critical observations of Italy's unequal wealth distribution; 20 percent of the population controlled 80 percent of the property.

Workload Scrutiny

You can identify how much of your time is devoted to tasks that are critical or valuable by performing workload scrutiny. To accomplish this, you can review your time log and your task list, distinguishing between the tasks that are valuable and the tasks that are critical. To scrutinize your workload, you can consider how much time you are devoting to each type of task.

Similarly, you can determine how much of your time is devoted to tasks that are neither critical nor valuable. These are nonessential tasks. When you scrutinize your workload, you can compare it to the 80/20 rule.

Time Estimation

Definition:

With practice, you can become adept at *time estimation,* or forecasting how much time a given activity will take. Document how much time an activity takes you the next three times you complete it; use the average of the three times to estimate how much time the activity should take in the future. Some time managers choose to add 20 percent on to their estimates of each activity, so that they do not overschedule themselves.

Example:

Alice, a new realtor, needs to estimate how long it will take her to show a house to prospective buyers. She documents the time it takes her to give three successive showings: 35 minutes, 40 minutes, and 60 minutes. Alice determines that she can estimate this task to take her 45 minutes, on average, in the future.

How to Analyze Tasks

A good analysis of your tasks includes a comprehensive list of the tasks that typically consume your day alongside your rating of each task's value and importance.

Guidelines

To analyze your current tasks, follow these guidelines:

- Compile a list of the tasks that consume your time on a typical day.
- Refer to your time log to be sure that you are accurately reporting the time spent on activities.
- Refer to your task list for the tasks rated "C".
- Refer to your task list for the tasks rated "V".
- Underline the tasks that are rated neither "V" nor "C".
- Review your task list, and write an "E" next to those that you consider enjoyable.
- Double-underline any of the tasks that are neither "V" nor "C" nor enjoyable.
- You have now analyzed each task and identified whether it is critical, valuable, enjoyable, or none of the these.

Example:

Bob, a forensic accountant, has written a list of all of the tasks that typically consume his day. He referred to his time log, and made sure he was accurately accounting for time spent on phone calls, emails, and interruptions.

Bob's tasks rated "C" included completing his case load and appointments with clients. Bob's tasks rated "V" included time spent collaborating with colleagues.

Bob identified some activities that are neither "V" nor "C", but are enjoyable, including lunch with friends. Bob also identified tasks that he considers neither "V", "C", nor "E", such as attending unproductive staff meetings.

DISCOVERY ACTIVITY 2-4

Analyzing Tasks

Scenario:

Karen is a teacher in a public school. She has great ideas for additional presentations she'd like to make in the classroom, but she finds it difficult to find enough time to incorporate new initiatives. Her principal frequently asks Karen to pitch in on fundraisers and committees on the weekends. She's considered a wonderful listener by many of the other teachers, who use Karen as a sounding board every afternoon. Karen has trouble finding time in the day for everything she wants to accomplish as well as everything that others expect of her.

1. **Karen has compiled a list of her daily tasks and now she wants to analyze them. What else does she need?**

    a) Karen needs her principal's input.

    b) Karen needs to consult with other teachers.

    c) Karen has everything she needs.

    d) Karen needs to consult her time log.

2. **How should Karen mark the tasks on her task list that are neither valuable, nor critical, nor enjoyable?**

    a) Karen should mark them with a "V".

    b) Karen should mark them with an "E".

    c) Karen should cross them out.

    d) Karen should double-underline them.

3. **True or False? Karen needs to analyze her current tasks. After Karen compiles a list of the tasks that consume her time, her next step should be reviewing her task list.**

    ___ True

    ___ False

DISCOVERY ACTIVITY 2-5

Discussing Time Analysis

Scenario:

Reflect on your time analysis, and consider the following questions.

1. Using the guidelines presented, create a time log. Using your time log to guide you, answer the following questions.

2. What kinds of tasks consume your time on a typical day? When you developed your time log, do you think you were able to accurately report the time that you spent on activities?

3. Which of your activities were critical? Which were valuable? Which were enjoyable? Did any of your activities fail to meet one of these categories? If so, do you think you might consider curtailing this activity in the future? Why or why not?

4. What do you think about analyzing your tasks in terms of their value? Have you thought about evaluating your activities in this way before? How will this affect your energy allocation?

5. Have you encountered the 80/20 rule before? How does it influence how you will assess your allocation of time and energy? Do you find yourself spending the bulk of your available resources on nonessential tasks? How can the 80/20 rule help you to spend your time and energy more wisely?

6. How adept are you at time estimation? Can you think of an instance when estimating your time accurately proved to be a valuable skill? If you have difficulty estimating the time needed for various tasks, how do you think you can use the information here to improve?

Topic C

Analyze Time Usage

Analyzing your time usage will help you to pinpoint how you are currently spending your time effectively and how you are spending it ineffectively. In this topic, you will analyze time usage.

The benefit of analyzing your time usage is that it will arm you with knowledge that will allow you to make more informed, strategic choices about how to spend your time.

Time Analysis

Definition:

Time analysis is the act of making judgments about your current use of time, so that you can make better informed choices in the future. Time analysis requires you to think about, critique, and refine your use of time.

Example:

Dana, a self-employed graphic designer, feels that she could expand her small business if she could find better ways to manage her time. She wants to complete a time analysis in order to critique and refine her use of time so that she can make better choices about her use of time in the future.

Sources of Distraction

Sources of distraction can be external, or caused by other people. These include phone calls, emails, colleagues asking for help, supervisors interrupting your work, or customers who need your attention.

Sources of distractions can be internal, if you distract yourself. You create internal distractions when you waste your own time, pass up opportunities to be productive, or postpone critical or valuable tasks.

Cost vs. Benefits of Activities

The cost of each activity refers to the time and energy that you devote to it. Every activity also has a benefit. Benefits may be monetary rewards (such as a paycheck), emotional rewards (such as relaxation), enrichment (such as professional or educational value), or goal attainment. Some activities may cost you greatly, but offer very little benefit.

How to Analyze Time Usage

A good analysis of your time results in the creation of a list of your premier time wasters. For the activities on your task list, create a chart with "cost" and the numbers 1 through 10 noted along the top, and "benefit" with the numbers 1 through 10 in a column down the left side. Chart each activity on a scale of 1 to 10 for cost, with 10 being those that consume the most time and energy. Now, chart each activity's benefit on a scale of 1 to 10, with 10 being those that carry the greatest rewards.

Lesson 2

Guidelines

To analyze your current time usage, follow these guidelines:

- Make sure you have your cost-benefit chart available.

- Note the activities that have the greatest cost and the greatest benefit. Highlight these activities with a different color pen.

- Note the activities that have the greatest cost and the lowest benefit. Highlight these activities with a second color pen.

- Cross-reference the high cost, low benefit activities with your task list so that you can see which activities are offering the most and least benefits.

- Identify those high cost, low benefit activities that are also not valuable, not critical, and not enjoyable. These are your premier time wasters.

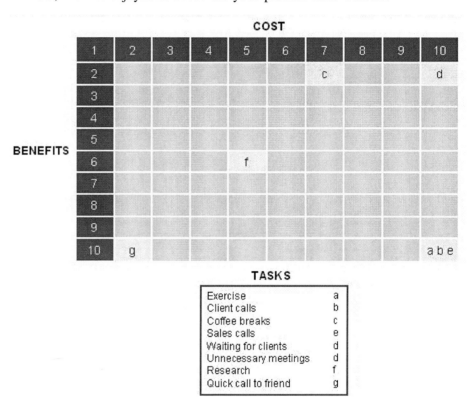

Figure 2-3: *A sample cost vs. benefits chart.*

Example:

David, a chef in a restaurant, had already created his cost-benefit chart. He noted the activities that have the greatest cost and the greatest benefit. He highlighted these with a green highlighting pen.

He also noted the activities that have the greatest cost and the least benefit. David highlighted these activities with a yellow highlighting pen.

He cross-referenced these high cost, low benefit activities with his task list, and he had identified them as not valuable, not critical, and not enjoyable. David pinpointed these activities as his premier time wasters.

DISCOVERY ACTIVITY 2-6

Analyzing Time

Scenario:

Sheila, an administrative assistant for a team of architects, has a tendency to take on more tasks than she can feasibly accomplish. She has difficulty saying "no" to anyone in the department. She also has trouble prioritizing her tasks, and sometimes the most important tasks are set aside in favor of nonessential activities, such as decorating the office for employees' birthdays. At the end of the week, Sheila wonders where the hours in each day went, and why she wasn't as effective as she wanted to be.

---

1. Sheila wants to analyze her time usage. She needs to identify how her time is wasted. Which activities are likely to be her most problematic time wasters?

    a) Activities that are critical.

    b) Activities that have high cost and low benefits and are neither valuable, critical, nor enjoyable.

    c) Activities that are enjoyable but low cost.

    d) Activities that are valuable only to Sheila.

---

2. If Sheila wants to analyze her time usage, what does she need to have readily available?

    a) Her cost-benefit chart

    b) An itemized list of her vacation days from the last year

    c) A spreadsheet of her time for the last year

    d) A clock or watch

---

3. True or False? Activities that are high cost, low benefit, and not valuable, not critical, and not enjoyable are most likely time wasters.

    ___ True

    ___ False

DISCOVERY ACTIVITY 2-7

Discussing Time Usage

Scenario:

Reflect on your time usage, and share your ideas in the group discussion.

1. Using the guidelines presented, analyze your time usage.

2. When you analyzed your time usage, which of your activities did you find to have the greatest cost and the greatest benefit? Which of your activities have the greatest cost and the lowest benefit? Were there any surprises for you when you analyzed your time usage?

3. What were some of the premier time wasters that you identified? Did any of these surprise you? Were you previously aware that these activities are unproductive? Do you think you might consider curtailing these activities in the future? Why or why not?

4. What are some of the sources of distraction in your life? How have you tried to address them?

5. What is your opinion of the guidelines for analyzing your current time usage? Was it interesting and helpful to you to find out how you are spending your time?

6. Based on the exercise of analyzing your time usage, what changes do you think you might make in your behavior? What did you learn or observe about your use of time that surprised you?

TOPIC D

Analyze Energy Flow

Being aware of the most productive and least productive times of your day will help you to work most effectively. In this topic, you will analyze your energy flow.

You want to know where your energy is being expended so that you can find more effective ways of channeling it. By analyzing your energy flow, you can capitalize on the times of day that are most productive for you, and leverage those influences that prove energizing to you. You can also find ways to maximize momentum and reduce burnout.

Daily Energy Cycle

Everyone is different; each person's high points and low points in their energy cycles will occur at different times of the day.

As your cycle begins, you have energy.

You begin working, and use energy.

You tire.

Your energy depletes.

You refresh yourself with food, rest, or adrenaline.

Your energy rises, and you return to your activities.

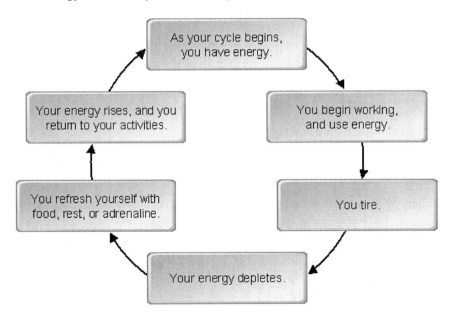

Figure 2-4: *The daily energy cycle.*

LESSON 2

Personal Energy Sources

Definition:

Every person has *personal energy sources,* which are the factors that refresh, revitalize, and motivate you. Your personal energy sources are what make you "tick," and they are as unique as you are. Your personal energy sources can be external, such as the motivation provided by a paycheck, a deadline, or a demanding client. They can also be internal, such as a drive to succeed or a feeling of job satisfaction.

People recharge their energy in different ways. Some people derive energy from taking a break to get fresh air, taking a coffee or conversation break with colleagues, or going for a walk.

Example:

Anna, a television producer, has pinpointed several personal energy sources. She thrives on a hectic schedule, and feels more energetic when she's surrounded by a lot of activity and people. Anna is motivated by the pressure of deadlines, and she seems to feel more energetic on bright, sunny days.

Momentum and Burnout

You can achieve and capitalize on your *momentum,* or the strength and energy gathered from productive events. When you achieve momentum, you will feel that you could continue at an energetic pace indefinitely. You can create momentum by capitalizing on your successes; when you are energized and productive, make a note of the factors that have led you to that moment.

We can also suffer from *burnout,* or the exhaustion and energy depletion caused by working too hard and too long. None of us can be effective continually without replenishing our personal energy. For some people, boredom leads to burnout; for others, being overscheduled and overworked leads to burnout. Avoid burnout by making a note of the factors that lead you to feel exhausted and depleted, so that you can avoid or minimize them.

How to Analyze Energy Flow

A good analysis of your energy flow includes a concise description of your most energetic and effective times of the day.

Guidelines

To analyze your energy flow, follow these guidelines:

- Write down your most significant personal energy sources.
- Make sure you have your time log available. On your time log, refer to the starred items. These are your times of greatest productivity.
- Compare your personal energy sources with your times of greatest productivity to identify the highlights of your energy cycle.
- Note periods of momentum or burnout, and note the events that preceded each.
- Write a concise description of your most energetic and effective times of day.

Example:

George, a copy editor, wants to analyze his energy flow. He creates a list of all of his most significant personal energy sources. He refers to his time log, and notes his times of greatest productivity.

He compares his personal energy sources with his times of greatest productivity in his daily energy cycle. George is able to write a concise description of his most energetic and effective times of the day, which are the hours between the early morning and early afternoon.

DISCOVERY ACTIVITY 2-8

Analyzing Energy Flow

Scenario:

Rhonda is a bank manager who seems to have difficulty channeling her personal energy. She wakes in the morning feeling tired. She usually feels sluggish every afternoon at work, but in the evenings, her energy is replenished and she is able to be productive for several more hours at night. She thinks of herself as a "night owl," and goes to bed very late. Rhonda drinks coffee all day, but it doesn't seem to help her feel better. She doesn't know why others seem to have energy throughout the day.

1. **Rhonda wants to analyze her energy flow. How should she begin?**

    a) Rhonda should first focus on getting more sleep.

    b) Rhonda should ask other bank managers how they manage their time.

    c) Rhonda should first make a list of her personal energy sources.

    d) Rhonda should focus on her critical activities and not worry about her lack of energy.

2. **When analyzing energy flow, what does Rhonda need to refer to on her time log?**

    a) Rhonda needs to refer to the starred tasks.

    b) Rhonda needs to refer to the critical tasks.

    c) Rhonda needs to refer to the enjoyable tasks.

    d) Rhonda needs to refer to the underlined tasks.

3. **True or False? The final step in analyzing your energy flow is writing down your most significant personal energy sources.**

    ___ True

    ___ False

DISCOVERY ACTIVITY 2-9

Discussing Energy Flow

Scenario:

Consider the following questions regarding energy flow, and share your ideas in the group discussion.

1. Using the guidelines presented, analyze your energy flow.

2. What are some of your most significant personal energy sources? What are the times of the day when you are more energetic and productive?

3. What are some of the highlights of your personal energy cycle? Have you ever tried to capitalize on these productive times in the past? How effective do you think you are at leveraging your most productive daily time periods?

4. What is your opinion of the guidelines for analyzing your energy flow? Did you find these guidelines instructive and helpful? Why or why not?

5. What kinds of experience have you had with momentum and burnout? Do you find these factors to be influential in your life? How do you like to capitalize on your momentum? How do you minimize the effects of burnout?

6. How do your personal energy sources help you function effectively? Are there additional sources of energy that you could be using? In your opinion, do highly effective people have more personal energy sources than less effective people?

Lesson 2 Follow-up

In this lesson, you analyzed your allocations of energy and time.

1. Reflect on the importance of identifying how your energy is being spent. Were there surprises for you about how you currently use your energy?

2. Consider the benefits of keeping a time log. How did collecting data about your time usage change your perceptions?

NOTES

LESSON 3
Identifying Personal Style

Lesson Objectives:

In this lesson, you will identify elements of your personal work style that contribute to your effective use of time.

You will:

*   Review a successful day or project.
*   Analyze your preferences.
*   Identify your personal strengths.
*   Identify your personal motivators.
*   Identify methods of reducing time wasters.

LESSON 3

Introduction

Every person has a unique personal style that includes preferences about work and organizational techniques that affect their use of time. In this lesson, you will identify your personal style so that you can identify personal motivators and personal strengths; in the context of time management, this is significant because it will help you to be as effective as possible.

Identifying your personal style will help you capitalize on your strengths, leveraging the influences that help you achieve your greatest productivity, and downplay the effects of any detractors, such as the factors that deplete your energy.

TOPIC A

Review a Successful Day or Project

We can all think of a past success: a project that went well, or a day when we felt particularly effective and productive. You can use your past successes as blueprints for making improvements in your time management efforts. As you reflect on a past success, you can note what worked well for you before, how you worked effectively, what tools and techniques were helpful to you, and you can capitalize on those positive experiences as you move forward in the time management process.

One of the ways that you can improve your performance in the future is by benchmarking a time in your life when you considered your time management to have been a success. You want to reflect on a successful day or a successful project and use that memory of success as a guiding light when embarking on future efforts.

Success

Definition:

Success is attaining a desired outcome. There are professional and personal successes.

Success comes in different forms and may relate to different parts of your life.

Type of Success	Description
Professional success	Attaining a desired level of professional achievement, reaching a work-related goal, or satisfying your employer's business requirements. Professional success is frequently defined by your employer.
Personal success	Attaining your desired level of achievement in leisure time pursuits, reaching a personal goal, or satisfying your own ambitions. Personal success is defined by each person, depending on your personal goals and values.

Example:

> C.J. and Jamie are salespeople working for the same car dealership. Their employer has mandated certain definitions of professional success for them: they must achieve a certain sales quota each quarter, they must submit the appropriate paperwork for each car sold, and they must follow up with each customer according to the dealership's prescribed customer service protocol.
>
> But C.J. and Jamie have different definitions of personal success. C.J.'s definition of success includes achieving a happy balance between work and home life and winning triathlons. Jamie's definition of personal success includes reaching a desired level of financial security, so that a comfortable retirement is guaranteed.

How to Review a Successful Day or Project

A good review of a past successful day or project results in a clear, one-sentence description of the techniques or processes that worked well for you before, so that you can work more effectively in the future by leveraging those elements of success to your advantage.

Guidelines

To review a past success, follow these guidelines:

- Think of a past project, event, meeting, presentation, or even an entire day that was a success. This can be either a professional success or a personal success.

- As you reflect on that past success, write a brief description of it. If you prefer not to write at length, just jot down your ideas. Be sure that you:

  — Describe the particular event and its challenges.

  — Describe what you did to address those challenges.

  — Describe the specific steps you took that led you to be successful.

  — Describe what worked for you in that particular case: Did you prepare in a special way? Did you work differently on this project than you had in the past? Did you use special techniques that helped you succeed? Did you collaborate with anyone? Were there other factors working in your favor?

  — Describe the results of your efforts. What was the ultimate outcome of this past success?

- As you describe your past success, reflect on the following considerations:

  — Consider how this past success contributed to your professional life or your employer's business requirements.

  — Consider what feedback, if any, you received from others.

  — Consider what made you most proud about this past success.

  — Consider how this event contributed to your personal goals.

  — Consider the satisfaction you derived from this event.

  — Consider why this event was important to you.

  — Consider how you think you could replicate this successful event in the future. What were the tools, steps, and techniques that were most helpful to you at that time that you could use again in the future? What specific factors helped you succeed, and how can your capitalize on those next time?

- Using your answers to those questions as your guiding lights, write a brief description of the tools, techniques, or processes that worked well for you before and describe how you plan to incorporate them into your efforts at time management.

Example:

Kevin reflected on a past project, a major sales presentation to a group of customers, that he considered a success. He noted that he had prepared carefully by researching his topic and planning his presentation. Kevin had anticipated some of the questions he expected the customers to ask, and he practiced answering those questions in front of his coworkers.

Being well prepared for the presentation helped him feel confident and assured, and he was proud of his ability to deliver a great presentation. Kevin didn't achieve this alone; he asked for feedback on his performance from his coworkers, and incorporated their constructive criticism into his presentation. This particular success netted a sale for Kevin, which satisfied one of his employer's business requirements. Kevin's manager considered the results of his efforts to be hugely successful. He also received positive feedback from the customers.

Kevin knows that the next time he walks into a roomful of customers, he can use the same tools of advance preparation to ensure his success. Kevin has identified some of the techniques that worked well for him before, and he plans to use them again in the future. He knows that the advance preparation saved him time in the long run, as he was able to net a sale through one well-rehearsed presentation. This is part of his ongoing strategy of time management.

DISCOVERY ACTIVITY 3-1

Reviewing a Successful Day

Scenario:

Lauren is an events planner. During her busiest seasons, she finds it nearly impossible to meet all of her clients' demands. She wants to review one of her most successful days so that she can figure out what she's done well in the past and repeat that performance in the future.

1. **Lauren has come to you asking for your advice as she reflects on a past success. Which of the following would be among the steps she should take as she reflects on a past success?**

    a) She should consider a career path that suits her better.

    b) She should make a list of the things she's failed to accomplish.

    c) She should consider the preparations that she made in advance of her past successful event.

    d) She should make a list of the things she'd like to accomplish in the future.

2. As Lauren reflects on a past successful day or event, which of the following are among the considerations she should include?

   a) Lauren should consider why that past success was important to her.

   b) Lauren should consider how that past event contributed to her goals.

   c) Lauren should consider the feedback she received from others.

   d) Lauren should consider what she should have done differently at that time.

3. True or False? In thinking about her past success, Lauren has chosen to describe "a day off, with nothing at all on the agenda." This is an appropriate choice within the context of reflecting on a past success.

   ___ True

   ___ False

DISCOVERY ACTIVITY 3-2

Discussing a Past Success

Scenario:

Consider the following questions regarding past successes, and share your ideas during the group discussion.

1. Using the guidelines presented, reflect on a past success.

2. What was the past success that you chose to reflect on? What were some of the elements that led to your success? What were some of the special steps that you took to ensure success in that instance? What were some of the challenges you faced at that time, and how did you overcome them?

3. Prior to taking this course, have you spent time considering your past successes? How helpful did you find this exercise? How does reflecting on your past successes influence your thinking? Does it change how you will approach future challenges?

4. As you consider a past success, think about your effectiveness at replicating that success. What elements of that event have you been able to repeat? What elements of that successful event would you like to incorporate into your work life right now? How do you think that reflecting on past successful projects might boost your confidence or help you improve your productivity?

5. Is this your first experience with incorporating past successes into efforts at improved time management? How do you intend to use your past successes to your advantage in approaching time management? Conversely, do you think it might help you in your time-management efforts if you reflect on some of your past projects that were not very successful? Why or why not?

Topic B

Analyze Your Preferences

People who are extremely productive have figured out what charges their batteries, and they find ways to keep themselves energized and productive throughout the day. In this topic, you will analyze your preferences for remaining energized and focused on your goals.

You're an individual, and as such you have unique preferences about how you like to work and how you like to organize your materials. Do you prefer working alone in a quiet, neatly organized space, or do you thrive best when you're in the midst of a bustling office? Do you prefer working collaboratively with a team? Do you function well under the pressure of a deadline? All of these personal preferences help define what makes you effective. By analyzing your preferences, you can make decisions about how to be more effective throughout the day.

Personal World View

Definition:

Each of us holds a *personal world view*, or a unique perspective and philosophy about the world and our place in it. Your world view is influenced by your education, upbringing, religion or belief system, and values. Your world view affects how you interact with other people, how you think about your work, how you use your time, and how you approach problem solving. For the purposes of time management, reflecting on your personal world view will help you capitalize on the unique way that you approach all of these elements of work.

Example:

Peter, a research assistant, has a world view that reflects his unique perspective, education, and upbringing. Because he was raised by two mathematicians, Peter has learned to tackle problems with diligence and patience. After spending two years in the Peace Corps in Latin America, he has a tolerance for a chaotic, stressful environment. Since Peter is comfortable working patiently for long periods, he sometimes struggles with adjusting quickly to changes in his work environment. His unique world view affects Peter's use of time, his ideas about time, and his approach to time management.

Work Style

Definition:

A *work style* is a person's preferred way of working; it includes preferences regarding noise level, activity level and pace, physical environment, level of interaction with other people, and level of responsibility. A work style can incorporate any preferences that you have about your professional life, including how intensely you like to work, whether you prefer working independently or collaboratively, how much detail you like to attend to, how much supervision you prefer to have, and so on.

Example:

Brenda and Catherine are both excellent reporters, but their work styles are very different. Brenda's preferred work style includes working independently, developing her own story ideas, finding her own sources, and setting her own schedule. Brenda likes to work in a quiet office by herself, and she requires very little supervision or interaction with others. Brenda believes she produces her best work when she is left alone to think quietly, and she likes having plenty of lead time for each article.

Catherine's preferred work style includes working as part of a team of reporters investigating stories together, and she likes bouncing ideas off others. Catherine enjoys sharing creative ideas with her editor, she thrives on the energy presented by a busy, noisy editorial office, and she prefers to have short deadlines. Catherine likes having the option to work quietly if she feels like it, but most of the time she prefers to be surrounded by people. Both reporters have identified the work styles that work best for them, and they leverage those preferences into effective work habits.

Continuum of Styles

There is a continuum of preferences about work styles. Some people may find themselves at the far end of the continuum, and prefer to work independently and in a quiet environment all the time, while others like to work independently sometimes, in a quiet room sometimes, and within a bustling team at other times. While your work style may vary, depending on the task, it is helpful to identify your general preferences.

How to Analyze Your Work Style Preferences

A good analysis of your preferences will help you understand your preferred work style. Identifying your preferences will help you capitalize on the factors that make you more productive.

Guidelines

To analyze your preferences, follow these guidelines:

- Reflect on one day, or a certain period in your life, when you felt productive, energized, and enthusiastic about work.

- Review your analysis of your past success, and reflect on the elements that led to success.

- Note the details of the experience. Answer the following questions, including as much detail as you like:

  — Do you feel most energized and productive when you are working alone or when you are working in a group? Do you look forward to collaborating with a team? Do you relish the prospect of uninterrupted hours of independent work time?

— Do you prefer the pace of your work to be dictated to you, or prefer to manage your own pace?

— Do you like to be the person in control of a project or task, or do you prefer to allow someone else to take that responsibility? Are you most comfortable structuring your own work, or do you like it when someone else manages the parameters?

— Do you like to work on tasks that are assigned by others, or do you prefer to create your own assignments?

— How intensely do you like to work?

— How long do you like to work at one time?

— Do you enjoy attending to small details, or do you prefer focusing on the "big picture"?

— Are you most productive when you work steadily on one task at a time, or are you most productive when you are juggling several tasks?

— Do frequent interruptions energize you and keep you on your toes, or do they overwhelm and distract you?

— Do you feel most comfortable when your schedule is planned out in advance, or do you thrive on changes and surprises?

— If you could design your ideal work environment, what would it look like? What would be included in the work space?

   – Would it be a quiet space, or do you feel energized by background noise?

   – Would you prefer to work alone or with others? Is it important to you that you have people around to talk to?

   – Is it important to you to be able to look out a window? Is it important to you to be able to go outside during the work day?

   – Do you enjoy attending meetings with others, or do you find meetings tiring?

   – Is it important to you that your work space be uncluttered and neat?

   – Is it important to you that your schedule doesn't change from day to day? What would your ideal work schedule look like?

• Make any additional notes about your work style and preferences. Include other factors that energize you or elements of your work life that help you be more productive.

• Using your newfound self-knowledge, complete the following two sentences:

If I could design my own work environment, it would look, sound, and feel like this:

If I could structure my work life in any manner that I choose, I would choose to work in this way:

Example:

Jason wanted to analyze his personal work style so that he could find ways to leverage his preferences and make himself more productive. He reflected on a past day that was successful: he had effectively organized an annual meeting for 300 company employees and shareholders. He had managed all of the aspects of that corporate event, including reserving the meeting space and refreshments, planning the speakers, organizing attendance, and producing the annual report. Jason reviewed his analysis of that event, recalling the elements that worked to his advantage.

Jason had particularly enjoyed planning the annual meeting because he was given full responsibility for all of the small details, and he was able to work independently and take ownership of the event. While Jason is willing to take direction from a supervisor, he feels that he is more productive when he can work independently.

Jason realized that when he was planning the details of the annual meeting, he was happily focused and energetic throughout the day. He felt great and was able to work intensely for long periods. However, he finds that whenever he has long meetings with other people, he feels bored, sluggish, and finds it hard to summon the energy to be productive. Jason realized that it's important to him that he be able to work independently. Jason also realized that he prefers a quiet, solitary work environment. By identifying what makes him tick, Jason can look for ways to leverage these personal preferences into a more productive work life.

DISCOVERY ACTIVITY 3-3

Analyzing Preferences

Scenario:

Ann is a middle manager for a large paper distributor. Her position requires her to work closely with various teams, including those employees that she supervises and those in upper management. Ann has a quiet personality, and frequently feels overwhelmed by the constant influx of people coming and going through her office door. She finds it exhausting to work closely with people all day and often finds herself feeling tired, sluggish, and ineffective at work. She notices that other managers seem to derive energy from working with groups of people, and wishes she were more extroverted.

1. **Ann wants to analyze her personal work preferences. What should she do first?**

   a) Analyze her preferences by working through the recommended questions.

   b) Write a two-sentence description of her work style and preferences.

   c) Try to be more outgoing on the job.

   d) Put a Do Not Disturb sign on her office door each day.

2. Ann has come to you asking for your help as she tries to analyze her work preferences. Which of the following is among the recommended questions that you would suggest she try to answer?

    a) Do you feel most energized and productive working alone or in a group?

    b) Do you prefer to work closely with one or more teammates?

    c) Do you like to work steadily on one task at a time, or do you prefer to juggle several tasks at once?

    d) What do you believe is the most successful way to work?

Discovery Activity 3-4

Discussing Work Style Preferences

Scenario:

Consider the following questions about work style preferences, and share your ideas during the group discussion.

1. Using the guidelines presented, analyze your work style preferences.

2. As you analyzed your work style preferences, what were some of the things you discovered about yourself? In what circumstances do you feel most energetic, productive, and enthusiastic about work? Do you prefer to work independently or collaboratively?

3. What are some of the elements of your work life that you would like to leverage more effectively? What would your ideal work space look, sound, and feel like? What would be the structure of your ideal workday?

4. As you reflect on your preferences, what have you learned about your work style? How do you plan to try to incorporate more of your preferences into your working life? How do you think that leveraging your preferences might make you more effective at work?

5. What are some of the work preferences you have that you have not yet found a way to incorporate into your current working life? Have you considered discussing with your supervisor some ideas for adapting your work environment to leverage your preferences? Why or why not?

6. Which of your work preferences are you already leveraging to your advantage? What suggestions would you make to another student of time management about how you've incorporated your preferences into your work life? What ideas have you had that have helped you become more productive using your preferences?

TOPIC C

Identify Personal Strengths

As a unique individual, you have personal strengths that you can leverage to achieve greater success. In this topic, you will identify your own strengths.

Each of us has personal strengths that are as different and unique as we are. You want to identify your personal strengths so that you can effectively capitalize on them, become more productive throughout the day, and make continued progress in your pursuit of improved time management.

Strengths

Definition:

Everyone has personal *strengths*, which are the positive qualities, attributes, personality traits, and inherent assets that help you to be a better, more effective worker. Any skills or abilities that you have can be considered strengths.

Example:

Sally, a newspaper editor, can identify several personal strengths that have served her well in her professional life. These positive inherent assets and personality traits include an ability to pay attention to details, an ability to concentrate for long periods of time, and a quiet, calm personality, which helps her keep her cool during times of crisis in the newsroom. These personal strengths serve her well in her position as an editor.

How to Identify Personal Strengths

A good description of your strengths includes a list of the personal qualities, attributes, and inherent assets that contribute to your effectiveness in your professional life. If you leverage your strengths, you can maximize your productivity.

Guidelines

To identify your personal strengths, follow these guidelines:

- Make a comprehensive list of the qualities and attributes that you have.
- Include any qualities and assets that others have praised you for in the past.
- Include any skills or abilities that have served you professionally.
- Include any assets that served you well during your education.

- Include any qualities that may contribute to your social life, even if they do not relate to your current job. You may have hidden strengths that you are not utilizing at work, and by recognizing them, you may be able to find new ways to utilize them throughout your day.

- Include any attributes that you have not yet had a chance to use in the workplace.

Example:

Jonathan, a payroll clerk, wrote out a comprehensive list of his strengths. He included the qualities and assets that he has, such as his ability to work well under pressure, and some personal qualities, such as friendliness, that others have praised him for in the past.

He included assets that have served him well in his professional life, such as a cheerful willingness to work hard. He also included assets that served him well in his education, such as a good memory and an attention to detail. Jonathan also included some assets that don't relate to his current position, and some attributes that he has not yet had a chance to use in the workplace, such as his skill at public speaking.

DISCOVERY ACTIVITY 3-5

Identifying Personal Strengths

Scenario:

Donna works as an administrative assistant to a team of doctors. She is well-liked by her coworkers and supervisors, and she has consistently received positive performance appraisals. She wants to make an inventory of her personal strengths, but she is having difficulty getting started.

---

1. **Donna has come to you to ask for help in creating her list of personal strengths. How would you advise her to begin?**

   a) Tell Donna to make a comprehensive list of her qualities and attributes.

   b) Tell Donna to make a comprehensive list of the qualities and attributes she most admires in others.

   c) Tell Donna to review her résumé and identify the positions she has most enjoyed.

   d) Tell Donna to ask her supervisor for positive feedback.

---

2. **Which of the following are among the recommended strategies for developing a good description of your personal strengths?**

   a) You should include the assets that others have praised you for in the past.

   b) You should include the abilities that have helped you in your professional life.

   c) You should include the skills and abilities that you would like to develop in the future.

   d) You should include the assets and abilities that you have not yet put to use in the workplace.

---

3. True or False? When developing your list of personal strengths, it's appropriate to include the qualities that contribute to your social life, even if they do not relate to your current job.

___ True

___ False

DISCOVERY ACTIVITY 3-6

Discussing Strengths

Scenario:

Consider the information presented about strengths as you review the following questions, and share your ideas within the group discussion.

1. Using the guidelines presented, identify your strengths.

2. What are some of the personal qualities and attributes that you identified? What are some of the skills, assets, and abilities that you have used in your professional life or during your education?

3. What are some of the personal strengths you identified that you have not yet had a chance to use in the workplace? Can you think of ways that you might be able to incorporate them into your working life?

4. What are some of the personal strengths that you have used to your advantage in the workplace? How have you effectively leveraged your strengths?

5. Can you think of any strengths that you have developed over time? Are there any strengths that didn't come naturally to you, but that you've worked hard to incorporate into your life? Are there any strengths that you are using in your current position that you hadn't had a chance to use in the past?

6. What are some of your hidden strengths? What are some of the qualities that you embody that you wish you could use more effectively in your working life? Do you have ideas for new ways that you could start leveraging your strengths more effectively on the job?

TOPIC D

Identify Personal Motivators

Each of us has personal motivators that influence how energetic we feel and how productive we are throughout the day. In this topic, you will identify your personal motivators so that you can leverage them to your advantage and further improve your management of your time. In this topic, you will identify personal motivators.

Some people are motivated by the pressing deadlines forced upon them; other people motivate themselves by creating artificial deadlines through procrastination. Different motivators work for different people. In this topic, you will identify your personal motivators so that you can leverage them to your advantage and find new ways to manage your time more effectively.

Motivators

Definition:

Motivators are the factors that provide people with the incentive and drive to act. Motivators are different for each of us, based on what's important to us. Motivators can be job-related or based on emotions. Internal motivators come from within the person; they're shaped by your personality and world view. External motivators come from outside sources, such as your employer, family, or peer group. Motivators can be positive, such as a hope for reward, or negative, such as a fear of losing employment. Motivators can be job-related, such as the promise of a raise, or based on emotions, such as a competitive streak.

Example:

Evan is a corporate trainer who has made a list of his motivators. Evan's motivators include enthusiasm for his work, a desire to excel and to please his superiors, and a hope for career advancement. Evan has a fear of failure and a fear of losing his financial status. In addition, his employer, his family, and his peer group have expectations for his behavior. All of these factors, whether they are positive, negative, internal, or external, are motivators for Evan; they give him the drive and incentive to act.

How to Identify Personal Motivators

A good description of your personal motivators includes a list of the factors that provide you with the drive and incentive to act. By identifying the motivators that work for you, you can leverage these factors and use them to your benefit as you improve your use of time at work.

Guidelines

To identify your personal motivators, follow these guidelines:

- Make a list of your personal motivators. These are the factors that provide you with the drive, incentive, or will to act. If you are not sure what your motivators are, you can begin by answering the following questions:

    — What do I hope to gain from working hard?

    — Why does it matter to me that I perform well at work?

    — Who are the people who have expectations for my behavior?

    — How do I plan to benefit from improving my use of time and becoming more productive?

    The answers to these questions will allow you to identify some of your motivators. You may have other motivators that provide you with the drive to act. As you continue to think about the factors that drive you, write down any additional motivators that you think of.

- Include the positive and negative factors that provide you with incentive.

- Include any internal and external motivators that drive you.

- Include the job-related motivators that provide you with incentive.

- Include the emotional factors that provide you with incentive.

Example:

Frances, a customer service representative, compiled a list of her personal motivators. To get started, she asked herself why she works hard in her job. She realized that she works hard because she wants to succeed in her career and she wants to be perceived as successful by others. She included positive factors, such as her wish to make more money, and negative factors, such as a fear of losing her job.

Some of her internal motivators include the satisfaction she takes in a job well done and her wish to get attention from others; she can capitalize on these motivators, because her company gives public recognition to the employees who excel. She also has external motivators, such as the motivation provided by her customers' demands, and the parameters for excellence that are defined by her supervisor.

Frances included some of her job-related motivators, such as the year-end bonus she might earn, her desire to be singled out for praise by top management, and the hope that she might be chosen as employee of the year. She also noted emotion-based motivators, such as her desire to please the customers and her desire to feel special.

DISCOVERY ACTIVITY 3-7

Identifying Personal Motivators

Scenario:

Grant is working in his first sales job. He enjoys the adrenaline rush of closing a sale, but finds it difficult to summon the necessary energy for less exciting tasks, such as making cold calls and developing prospects. As a result, he spends a large portion of his work day visiting with officemates and taking long breaks, and is not as consistently productive as he wants to be. He is not sure how other salespeople maintain their energy and productivity throughout the day. Although he is motivated by the incentive of commissions, he wants to identify additional motivators that he can leverage to his advantage.

1. **Grant has asked you to help him identify some of his personal motivators. What would you ask him to do first?**

    a) You would ask him to stop wasting his time during the work day.

    b) You would ask him to put a motivational sign near his desk that will remind him to keep working.

    c) You would ask him to make a list of all the personal motivators that he can think of.

    d) You would ask him to ask some more experienced salespeople for their advice.

2. **Which of the following are among the steps that Grant should take to identify his personal motivators?**

    a) He should list the positive influences that provide him with incentive.

    b) He should list any internal factors that give him motivation.

    c) He should list the influences that have provided motivation to famous people throughout history.

    d) He should list the emotional factors that provide him with incentive.

3. **True or False? Personal motivators can be any factors that provide you with the drive and incentive to act.**

    ___ True

    ___ False

DISCOVERY ACTIVITY 3-8

Discussing Motivators

Scenario:

Reflect on the questions below regarding motivators, and share your ideas during the group discussion.

1. Using the guidelines presented, identify your personal motivators.

2. What are some of the personal motivators you identified? What are some of the positive factors that motivate you? What are some of the negative factors that motivate you?

3. What are some of the personal motivators that have served you well throughout your working life? Have you ever had to try to find new sources of motivation on the job?

4. What are some of the positive factors that provide you with incentive? What are some of the negative factors? Have you ever tried to come up with additional incentives to keep yourself motivated? How successful have you been in leveraging your motivators to your advantage?

5. What are your motivators for improving your time-management process? Are your motivators powerful enough to change your behavior, or do you need to find additional motivational factors? Are there people in your working life who provide you with motivation on the job? Do you rely on other people to provide motivation, or are your motivating factors internal?

TOPIC E

Reduce Time Wasters

Reducing unwelcome time wasters is one of the most important elements of the process of time management. In this topic, you will identify the factors that waste your time and identify some effective strategies that you can use to reduce time wasters on the job.

In order to reduce the amount of time that you spend on activities that are not meaningful to you, you need to identify where your time is being wasted. You want to reduce the internal time wasters that you create for yourself as well as the external time wasters that other people create for you.

Internal Time Wasters

Definition:

Internal time wasters are the factors that both waste your time and are self-created or within your control. Internal time wasters could be part of your personality, such as a personal tendency to procrastinate or an unwillingness to tackle difficult chores. Internal time wasters vary for each person, and some people create more internal time wasters for themselves than others.

Example:

Stacy, a manager of a small team, has identified some of her internal time wasters. She recognizes her tendency to avoid tasks that she finds unpleasant or difficult, such as mediating disputes among employees. Stacy prefers to avoid confrontation in the workplace, so she procrastinates when she has to critique or correct an employee's behavior, which leads to poor employee performance. Stacy also tends to spend more time than necessary on fun projects she enjoys, leaving insufficient time for the ordinary chores and tasks that make up her workday. As a result of these internal time wasters, Stacy is not the effective manager that she wants to be.

Effective Internal Strategies

You can use a variety of strategies to reduce internal time wasters.

Internal Time Waster	Strategy
Procrastination	Create a rewards system; reward yourself for each task that you accomplish.
Unwillingness to tackle difficult chores	Break each chore down into a series of smaller tasks, working your way through difficult jobs step by step.
Wasting your own time	Use your list of personal motivators. Leverage those motivators so that they continue to work for you throughout the day.

External Time Wasters

Definition:

External time wasters are the factors that both waste your time and are created by other people or are beyond your control. External time wasters include interruptions; they distract you from valuable, critical, or enjoyable activities. They may be created by coworkers, supervisors, customers, friends, and even strangers.

Example:

Frank is an accountant who can identify several external time wasters. His supervisor interrupts him repeatedly throughout the day with questions that could easily be dealt with all at once. Frank also works within a loud office environment, where many of his colleagues provide external time wasters in the form of distractions and noisy interruptions. One of Frank's daily external time wasters is the parade of well-intentioned colleagues who drop by his office to chat, distracting him. Frank also has a client who fails to meet his deadlines on time, delaying Frank further.

Effective External Strategies

You can try using different strategies to reduce your problematic external time wasters.

External Time Waster	Strategy
Interruptions from supervisors and coworkers	Enlist their help. Ask to meet once daily to discuss issues, and then work without interruption. Post a sign that says, "Please Do Not Disturb." Set the instant message feature on your computer to "Please Do Not Disturb."
Distractions from colleagues	Develop an arsenal of polite responses, such as "I'm sorry I can't talk right now; I need to finish this project," or "I'm really focused on this task; do you mind if we get together at lunch instead?"
Daily interruptions	Chunk your tasks together. For example, you could choose to set aside a certain half-hour in the morning and a half-hour in the afternoon to return phone calls and email.
Extraneous noise	Use earplugs or headphones while you work.

How to Reduce Time Wasters

A good description of strategies for reducing time wasters includes a list of the strategies that you plan to use and your ideas for incorporating them into your improved time-management process.

Guidelines

To list effective strategies for reducing time wasters, follow these guidelines:

- Review the criteria for internal and external time wasters. Make a list of the troublesome time wasters that you face.

- Consider the recommended strategies for reducing time wasters. You can adopt these strategies or think of your own. Different strategies will work better for different people; you can try more than one strategy as you implement improvements.

- Write down one idea for addressing each time waster.

- Leverage your personal motivators.

  — If you are motivated by the promise of financial gain, post pictures in your work space of the things you hope to buy; maintain a list of the things you want to save up for, or display a picture of the ultimate reward, such as a vacation destination or new car.

  — If you are motivated by the desire to please your supervisor, ask for feedback when you've done well. Keep a "kudos" file of the praiseworthy performance evaluations or customer feedback you have received. Display any awards or distinctions that you have earned.

  — If you are motivated by others' success, display meaningful motivational quotes near your work space. Maintain a file of news clippings about others who have succeeded in your field. Display pictures of the successful people you admire to remind yourself of their example.

  — If you are a people person, team up with a buddy to help you work on a task, or find a mentor who can offer you advice and guidance as you approach challenging projects.

  — If you are motivated by a desire to please others and solve problems, you can recast any task in your mind as if it is a problem that a client is bringing to you for help. Look at your task in this new light, and help yourself solve it as if you were helping someone else.

Example:

Chris, a sales manager, made a list of her troublesome time wasters. They included a constantly ringing phone and a supervisor who interrupts her, as well as a personal tendency to avoid difficult chores. She considered the recommended strategies for reducing time wasters.

Chris wrote down one idea for reducing each time waster. She'll turn off her phone for regular periods while she attends to quiet work and return calls later in organized batches. She'll ask for the supervisor's cooperation in reducing the number of daily interruptions. And she will warm up each day with easy tasks, and then tackle her more difficult projects.

Chris leveraged her personal motivators, including her desire to succeed in the business world and a hope for financial gain. She posted a sign in her work space with the dollar amount that she hopes to earn in bonuses. She put a calculator on her desk so that she could quickly add up her daily and weekly commissions. And she created a rewards system for herself, treating herself to a reward every time she completed an unpleasant task.

DISCOVERY ACTIVITY 3-9

Reducing Time Wasters

Scenario:

Danielle prides herself on working hard, and as a result, she has been promoted several times during the past 10 years. With each promotion, she finds herself working longer hours and taking less vacation time. Danielle is proud of her professional accomplishments, but she has neglected her personal pursuits and now she wants to find a better balance between her work time and her personal time. Danielle struggles with time wasters that are both internal and external, and she wonders how she can combat her time wasters and become more balanced.

1. Danielle needs to find effective strategies for reducing time wasters, and she has come to you asking for your advice. What would you tell her to do first?

    a) Tell Danielle to ask everyone to leave her alone during the work day.

    b) Tell Danielle to make a to-do list each morning and accomplish everything on it.

    c) Tell Danielle to review her list of personal motivators.

    d) Tell Danielle to focus first on her work, and then focus on her personal life in her spare time.

2. Which of the following are among the recommended strategies that Danielle could consider?

    a) Danielle could consider enlisting the help of her coworkers and supervisors.

    b) Danielle could consider developing polite responses to interruptions.

    c) Danielle could consider taking a demotion so that she has a more manageable job.

    d) Danielle could consider chunking similar tasks together.

3. True or False? For each problematic time waster, there is one specific strategy that should work for everyone.

    ___ True

    ___ False

DISCOVERY ACTIVITY 3-10

Discussing Time Wasters

Scenario:

Reflect on the following questions regarding time wasters, and share your ideas during the group discussion.

1. Using the guidelines presented, identify your troublesome time wasters.

2. What are some of the troublesome time wasters that you identified? What are some of the strategies you have decided to use to address your time wasters?

3. Have you tried to address your time wasters in the past? If so, what strategies did you use? How successful have you been?

4. Sometimes, our most difficult time wasters are those caused by other people. How have you tried to address time-wasting issues caused by others? How did the other people respond to you? If your experience was less than satisfactory, how would you approach this differently in the future?

5. For some people, reducing time wasters at work is a new prospect. Had you ever tried to actively reduce your time wasters before? What are some of the strategies that you've found most effective? What are some of the strategies that you plan to try for the first time?

Lesson 3 Follow-up

In this lesson, you identified some of the elements of your personal work style that contribute to your effective use of time.

1. Consider the importance of analyzing your personal preferences. How do you anticipate using this newfound self-knowledge to your advantage in the future?

2. Reflect on your personal strengths and how you might leverage them to your advantage. How does this change the way you think about your ability to use time effectively?

LESSON 4
Assembling the Toolbox

Lesson Objectives:

In this lesson, you will assemble a collection of time-management tools and strategies that you can use to take control of your time.

You will:

*   Identify strategies for negotiating for success.
*   Identify tasks to delegate.
*   Choose tools that work for you.

LESSON 4

Introduction

Effective time managers use a variety of techniques and strategies to achieve their goals. In this lesson, you will explore various negotiating skills and delegating skills that will help you manage your time; and you will identify ways to achieve diplomatic resolutions and to block out time and space for your own needs. You will assemble a toolbox of skills that will help you manage your time more effectively.

Assembling an array of effective time-management tools will help you to manage your time better. By identifying and implementing new strategies, you will be better equipped to address any time-management issues as they arise.

TOPIC A

Negotiate for Success

There are times when you are able to satisfy someone else's needs and requirements only by putting your own needs aside. Truly effective time managers are able to negotiate solutions whereby they meet their own needs as well as the other person's. In this topic, you will define negotiating for success.

Sometimes, you must negotiate for success by working with other people to agree on solutions that are feasible. You want to identify helpful strategies for time management so that you can accomplish everything that you need to, and also satisfy other people's expectations.

Requirements

Definition:

> In the context of time management, *requirements* are the essential or necessary actions you must take to complete a task or fulfill an obligation. Requirements may be established for you by a supervisor, or they may be mutually agreed upon between yourself and your colleagues, family, or friends. If your tasks do not meet the criteria of requirements, then they are nonessential, and you may consider curtailing or abandoning them.

Example:

> Adam, a recruiter, sometimes finds it difficult to attend to his to-do list. By reviewing his list of tasks, he realizes that some of the tasks are stated requirements of his job, including reviewing résumés and conducting interviews with potential candidates. These have been defined by his employer as requirements. Other tasks, such as reading trade journals and taking coffee breaks with colleagues, are rewarding, but are not required by his supervisor. Adam decides to focus on the job requirements defined by his employer and reconsider whether he needs to devote as much time and energy to nonessential tasks.

Diplomatic Solutions

Definition:

Diplomatic solutions are politely negotiated, mutually beneficial resolutions to time conflicts. A diplomatic solution meets your needs as well as the other person's, and it offers an alternative resolution to a time-related issue or problem. A diplomatic solution may require some compromise on either side of the conflict.

Example:

David's supervisor, Marvin, has asked him to stay late at work on Monday and attend a last-minute team meeting. But David had already scheduled a meeting with a vendor Monday evening to review a proposed project. Both meetings are important, so David decides to offer a diplomatic solution to this conflict. He asks Marvin if the team meeting could be rescheduled for early Tuesday morning, instead of Monday, so that he can participate in both events. This solution requires compromise from both parties: David will need to attend both a late meeting Monday and an early meeting Tuesday, and Marvin will have to reschedule his event.

The Diplomatic "No"

Effective time management may require you to turn down some activities, and saying "no" diplomatically is an important time-management tool. Practice delivering diplomatic refusals, such as, "I'm sorry, but I can't take on another project," or, "I'm sorry, but I need to focus on other priorities." Remember that a firm, polite refusal is often more helpful to the other person than a half-hearted acceptance.

Situation	Diplomatic Refusal
A request for volunteering	"I'm sorry, but I just can't take on any additional commitments this year."
A request to sit on a committee at work	"It sounds interesting, but I need to focus my energy on my job requirements this quarter."
A request to participate in an activity you're not interested in	"Thank you for the invitation, but I'm going to have to say no. I have too many other commitments."
A request to help a colleague with a project	"I'm flattered that you thought of me, but I need to focus all of my energy on the projects I already have."

Blocks of Time and Space

To be effective, you need to carve out blocks of time and space for yourself so that you can focus on the activities that are critical, valuable, or enjoyable for you. At work, you may be able to alert colleagues that you will be unavailable for certain time periods of the day, or hang a "do not disturb" sign near your workspace for brief periods. Consider arriving at work 30 minutes early to allow yourself a block of uninterrupted quiet time.

At home, you can negotiate with family members for certain times during the day or week when you will be free to focus on your own activities. Consider identifying quiet periods of the day, such as the early morning or late evening, when it may be easiest to carve out uninterrupted time.

Interruption Control

Some technological advances that are intended to make life easier may sometimes bring unwelcome distractions. Take control of your time by controlling the daily interruptions you receive from phone, email, instant messages, and pagers. Identify techniques for using these tools to your advantage by setting boundaries for their use.

Technology	Technique
Phone	Take advantage of the voice mail feature, and return phone calls all at once rather than throughout the day. During periods of intensely focused work, you may prefer not to answer calls.
Email	Rather than allowing yourself to be interrupted on a constant basis throughout the work day, choose a few times to respond to email.
Instant messages	During busy periods, you may prefer not to allow yourself to be interrupted by instant messages. You can set your instant message feature to "do not disturb" during such periods.
Pagers	If you are not relying on your pager to alert you to emergencies, consider turning it off when you need quiet concentration time.

How to Negotiate for Success

A good description of strategies that will help you negotiate for success outlines how you can reach diplomatic solutions to time-management problems.

Guidelines

To identify helpful negotiating strategies, follow these guidelines:

- Make a list of your three most frequent time-management problems.

- For each problem on the list, write down one possible technique for negotiating a solution.

  — If your issues relate to your tendency to take on too many tasks and activities, outline your plans for saying "no" diplomatically the next time you want to refuse a request.

  — If your problems stem from a supervisor assigning you too many tasks at once, write down your ideas for the helpful diplomatic solution that you plan to offer to your supervisor the next time this issue arises.

  — If you have difficulty juggling phone calls, email, and instant messages, outline your plans to implement new strategies for controlling those interruptions.

— If your problems stem from a conflict between your family obligations and your personal activities, outline your plans for negotiating an agreement with your family members.

Example:

Jane, the owner of a telemarketing firm, is trying to engineer the buyout of another, smaller firm; she also serves on several non-profit boards as a volunteer. She was facing time-management issues and needed to identify some helpful negotiating strategies. She began by making a list of her three most frequent time-management problems.

She struggles with taking on more projects than she wants to. She outlined her plans for saying "no" diplomatically, and wrote out what she might say the next time someone asks her to chair a community fundraising project. She also wrote down ideas for diplomatic solutions, such as how she might respond when colleagues ask to schedule time on her calendar when her schedule is already tight.

Jane also wants to achieve a better balance between her work life and her personal pursuits. She outlined her plans for negotiating a mutually beneficial arrangement with her family members and her plans to approach a relative with a shared childcare plan, so that she will have an evening each week to pursue her interest in classical piano. Jane also wrote down her ideas for controlling interruptions at work by implementing new controls for her phone, email, and instant message usage.

DISCOVERY ACTIVITY 4-1

Negotiating for Success

Scenario:

Larry, a team lead, wants to identify tools that he can use to negotiate for success. He considers himself a productive worker, but he has difficulty on the days when he is interrupted frequently. He likes to think of himself as the consummate team player, and he doesn't feel comfortable in refusing any extra work that is given to him by his boss or his coworkers. As a result, Larry often feels that his time is not within his control, and his own work suffers while he's busy helping his colleagues and mentoring less-experienced staffers. Larry's manager, Dana, is very frustrated that Larry always seems to have plenty of time to help everybody else, but he misses his own deadlines.

1. **Larry has come to you for advice regarding some of the negotiating tools that he wants to develop. What would you suggest that Larry should do first?**

   a) Larry should begin by refusing all new requests for help.

   b) Larry should begin by closing the door of his office each day until all his work is done.

   c) Larry should begin by making a list of his most frequent time-management problems.

   d) Larry should begin reminding Dana that he's well-liked by the staff and his heart is in the right place.

2. Larry is weighing his options. Which of the following techniques are part of the recommended strategy for negotiating time-management success as they have been defined here?

   a) Larry should first list his frequent time-management issues.

   b) Larry should write down some possible strategies for addressing his identified time-management issues.

   c) Larry should ask his colleagues for their helpful suggestions.

   d) Larry should research time-management strategies on the Internet.

3. True or False? If Larry is uncomfortable refusing extra activities that he doesn't have time for, then he should simply agree to do them anyway.

   ___ True

   ___ False

DISCOVERY ACTIVITY 4-2

Discussing Negotiating Strategies

Scenario:

Reflect on the following questions regarding negotiating strategies, and share your ideas during the group discussion.

1. Using the guidelines presented, identify helpful negotiating strategies.

2. What are some of the most problematic time-management problems that you face regularly? Have you tried to address them in the past? If so, what kinds of strategies have you tried? Are there any effective and unique strategies that you've developed that you can share?

3. What ideas have you had for incorporating diplomatic refusals on the job? Have you tried using diplomatic refusals? If so, how did people respond to you? Were you surprised if people responded well to your polite refusal or negotiation? How does the concept of diplomatic refusals influence your thinking about taking control of your own time?

4. Negotiating skills are a new behavior for some people. Are you developing negotiating skills for the first time? Does effective negotiation come easily to you, or do you have to work at it? What are some of the considerations that you like to keep in mind whenever you enter a negotiation with another person? Have you developed helpful ideas about negotiating skills that you can share with others?

TOPIC B

Delegate Tasks

Sometimes, your time is taken up by tasks and activities that could be done by someone else. In this topic, you will identify the importance and benefits of delegating tasks.

Your available time each day is divided among a number of tasks. It's possible that there are opportunities to save yourself time and energy by delegating some of those tasks to someone else. Identifying the appropriate delegation of tasks will make your workload more manageable.

Delegation

Definition:

Delegation is the act of empowering someone else to act for you. It means that you lessen your workload by handing off a task, project, activity, or responsibility. Managers delegate work when they assign projects to staff members. You delegate tasks to colleagues, family members, or friends when you ask them to take over something for you. You also delegate tasks when you hire someone to perform a chore for you.

Appropriate and Inappropriate Delegation

Delegation can be considered appropriate or inappropriate. Delegation is appropriate when you have the authority to hand off a task to another person, when the other person is equipped to handle the responsibility, or when you need extra help to handle the work. Within the business world, the parameters for appropriate delegation are defined by each employer, and may vary. Delegation may be appropriate when a less expensive or less constrained resource takes on a task. Delegation is inappropriate when you are handing off tasks without the authority to do so, when the other person is not equipped to handle the task, or when you don't need the extra help.

Example:

Bill is the leader of a team of volunteers. He decides to delegate some of the tasks, including fundraising and recruiting new members, to some of the other members of the team who have specialized experience. He asks Rosemary, an experienced development officer, to handle fundraising, and Bob, a personnel director, to handle recruitment. It is appropriate for Bill to delegate tasks to other volunteers because the other people are capable of doing the work, he can't accomplish everything by himself, and as the team leader, he has the authority to delegate.

LESSON 4

How to Delegate Tasks

A good analysis of tasks helps you to decide which tasks you can appropriately delegate.

Guidelines

To decide whether a task can appropriately be delegated, follow these guidelines:

- Make a list of the tasks, activities, and projects that you currently have responsibility for. For each item on the list, ask yourself the following questions to help you determine whether you can delegate it.

  — Is this a task that I must complete personally because I have specialized expertise?

  — Has my employer specifically entrusted this task to me?

  — Is completing it a stated condition of my employment?

  — Is this task part of my job description? Is it understood within my workplace team that I am the person responsible for this task?

  — If the answer to these questions is "yes," then it is not appropriate to delegate this task to someone else.

- Do I have the authority to delegate this task?

- Has my employer clearly given me the latitude to reassign this task to someone else?

  — If the answer to these questions is "no," then it is not appropriate to delegate this task to someone else.

- If I delegate this task, will I need to follow up on the other person's performance?

  — If the answer is "yes," then delegating this task may actually create additional work for you. Consider whether this will meet your objective of managing your time more effectively.

- Is there anyone who is ready and able to handle this task?

- If there is no one ready to take over this task now, is there anyone that I could train to take it over?

- Is it feasible to hire someone to do it?

Example:

Tina is a real estate lawyer and a partner in a firm employing more than 20 attorneys. She made a list of the tasks that she's responsible for, which include soliciting new business, meeting with clients, reviewing contracts, researching properties, scheduling her appointments, and advertising her firm's services. For each task on her list, she considered whether she had to do it herself, and whether she had the authority to delegate that task. Tina determined that there are some basic requirements of her job that she must complete personally.

Tina realized she had the authority to delegate some other tasks, including researching properties and scheduling her appointments. Some of the junior attorneys in her firm can research properties, and Tina's assistant can schedule her appointments without supervision.

Tina realized that she could train her proteges to take over some of the less important client meetings and review some simple, boilerplate contracts. She also decided to delegate the marketing duties by hiring an advertising company with specialized expertise to market her law firm's services.

DISCOVERY ACTIVITY 4-3

Delegating Tasks

Scenario:

Zachary is the executive director of a large library, and he has more administrative tasks on his agenda than he can possibly accomplish. Among his tasks are holding meetings with board members, lobbying for state funding, producing the library newsletter and other promotional publications, supervising staff and training volunteers, and soliciting donations from individuals and corporations. Zachary wants to delegate some of his responsibilities to others, but he is not sure which tasks are appropriate for him to delegate.

1. **Zachary has come to you asking for your advice on how to select tasks that would be appropriate to delegate to others. What would you tell him to do first?**

   a) Zachary should first accomplish the most important tasks himself, and then delegate the less important tasks to others.

   b) Zachary should first find volunteers who can help him with some of the work.

   c) Zachary should first ask the people on his staff which tasks they would like to take over.

   d) Zachary should first make a list of his tasks and responsibilities.

2. **One of the responsibilities that Zachary might consider delegating is the training of volunteers. As he considers this option, what are some of the questions he should ask himself?**

   a) Can someone else take responsibility for this task, or do I need to do it myself?

   b) Do I have the authority to delegate this task to someone else?

   c) Is there anyone who would enjoy taking over this task?

   d) If I work longer hours, is it possible that I can complete this task myself?

3. **True or False? Before Zachary delegates a task to someone else, he should consider whether he'll need to supervise the other person's performance.**

   ___ True

   ___ False

DISCOVERY ACTIVITY 4-4

Discussing Delegating

Scenario:

Reflect on the following questions regarding delegating, and share your ideas during the group discussion.

1. Using the guidelines presented, analyze your tasks to decide which tasks you can appropriately delegate.

2. What are some of the tasks you are currently responsible for? Are any of them specifically entrusted to you by your employer? Do you have the authority to delegate any tasks?

3. Have you tried delegating some of your tasks in the past? What have your experiences with delegating been like? Have you ever found that your attempt to delegate a task has met with resistance from the other person? How did you resolve that issue?

4. Had you ever before given conscious thought to appropriate versus inappropriate delegation? How do the recommended guidelines for judging appropriateness align with your experience? Have you ever had another person try to delegate tasks to you inappropriately? How did you respond? Why do you think it's necessary to have the authority to delegate a task? In your experience, what happens when people delegate tasks without authority?

5. Have you ever made a choice to train another person to take over a task for you? If so, did you consider this a form of delegation? In the final analysis, was it an effective time-saving step for you to take? How did the upfront investment in training time compare to the eventual benefit of handing off the task to someone else?

TOPIC C

Choose Tools that Work for You

There are many effective time-management tools, but not all of them will be helpful to every person. In this topic, you will identify some of the tools of time management, including to-do lists and calendars, and identify the tools that will suit your preferences, needs, and style. This will help you further refine your time-management skills.

Some time-management tools work well for some people but other people find them ineffective. You want to choose the tools that will suit your working style and personal preferences, so that you can use them to your greatest advantage to become more effective on the job.

Benchmarks

Definition:

A *benchmark* is a standard basis for comparison or evaluation. In the context of time management, benchmarks are created when you observe effective people who use their time well and copy their example by modeling your behavior after theirs. You can benchmark different performances, such as those of colleagues who are excelling on the job, famously successful people, or friends who are effective in fields other than your own.

Example:

Caroline, a realtor, wanted to try to improve her time management so that she could manage more clients and sell more houses. She identified two effective people to use as benchmarks: her supervisor at work and a successful doctor friend. Caroline asked them how they managed to structure their time so that she could learn from their example. Then she began to copy their behavior, modeling her use of time after theirs.

Caroline's benchmark of her supervisor showed her that she could save time by firmly controlling the time spent in meetings, beginning and ending each meeting as quickly as possible. By benchmarking her doctor friend's performance and modeling what she saw, she learned how to quickly, diplomatically end non-productive phone conversations with clients, thereby saving herself time.

Your Time's Monetary Value

Every hour of your time has a monetary value that can be determined by dividing your annual salary by 2,000, which is the standard number of hours worked at a full-time job in one year. Considering time's monetary value can help you decide how much time to spend on an activity. You may choose to spend less of your free time on non-productive activities, such as surfing the Internet or being idle.

Tools and Techniques: Pros and Cons

Consider time-management tools and techniques, including calendars, electronic planners, to-do lists, multitasking, deadlines, and prioritizing. Some people like calendars, which provide neat organization of deadlines and appointments; others dislike updating them. Some people like the satisfaction of completing to-do lists; others prefer addressing tasks as they arise. Some like to set deadlines for themselves, while others prefer not to create additional pressure. Use the tools or techniques that work for you.

Tool/Technique	Pros	Cons
Calendars and electronic planners	Calendars and electronic planners provide organization of deadlines and appointments.	Calendars and electronic planners require frequent updating. If you have multiple calendars (for example, one for work and one for home) it is easy for them to get out of sync.
To-do lists	To-do lists are useful because they allow you to see all your tasks at once.	Some people prefer to work on tasks as they arise. Most to-do lists don't allow you to rate the importance of any given task.
Deadlines	Self-imposed deadlines help some people feel in control of their time.	Some people prefer not to add to their own pressure by creating self-imposed deadlines.
Multitasking	Multitasking is an effective technique for some people who can concentrate on more than one task at once.	Multitasking doesn't work for every person or every situation. Some people are less effective when their attention is divided. Some tasks, such as face-to-face client meetings, require your undivided attention.
Benchmarking	Benchmarking allows you to learn from someone else's positive example.	Benchmarking may not be effective in every circumstance; for example, the person observed may use tools that would not suit your work style.
Prioritizing	Prioritizing allows you to work first on your critical and valuable activities. It will help you to attend to your long-term goals.	Prioritizing is difficult for some people, who erroneously end up prioritizing their schedules instead of scheduling their most important priorities.

The Myths of Multitasking

Multitasking is completing several tasks simultaneously. Contrary to popular belief, not everyone is capable of multitasking. Some people cannot effectively concentrate on more than one task at a time. And not every activity lends itself to multitasking; some activities will require your undivided attention.

How to Choose Tools that Work for You

A good analysis of the time-management tools that work for you results in the identification of the tools you plan to use.

Guidelines

To choose time-management tools, follow these guidelines:

- Consider your personal work style, your personality, your preferences, and the type of job you have, and how those factors mesh with time-management tools.

- If you are a detail-oriented person, you might like meticulously tracking your activities in a calendar.

- If you enjoy working independently and taking responsibility for your own projects, you may find that you like keeping track of your activities on a personal to-do list.

- If you thrive in a bustling workspace and you enjoy having lots of activities taking place around you, you might find that multitasking works well for you.

- If you are a very social and outgoing person and you enjoy working collaboratively, you may find that you are comfortable benchmarking others' performances and asking them to share their effective time-management tips.

- If you thrive on pressure, you may find that creating self-imposed deadlines is an effective time-management strategy for you.

- If you are a person motivated by a wish for financial gain, you might find that determining the monetary value of your time works well for you.

- As you work through your consideration of your preferences, reject the tools that you think will be ineffective for you because they don't suit your work style, personality, or preferences.

- Choose the tools that work well for you and identify ways that you plan to incorporate them into your time-management strategy.

- Consider any additional time-management tools that you have found to be effective and that you intend to use as part of your overall strategy of time management.

Example:

Pete, Dave, and John are purchasing agents in the same department who want to incorporate some time-management tools into their lives. They've considered their personal work styles and preferences, and how those factors will affect their use of time-management tools.

Pete is a detail-oriented, introverted person who enjoys working quietly by himself. He's decided to use calendars and to-do lists to keep track of his own activities. Dave is a very social and friendly person who is comfortable talking with anyone. He plans to benchmark his manager's use of time so that he can learn from that example.

John also enjoys working independently, but he's dyslexic and finds written instructions difficult, so he's decided against using calendars and to-do lists. John will create early deadlines to inspire himself to work more quickly.

DISCOVERY ACTIVITY 4-5

Choosing Tools that Work for You

Scenario:

Paula is a physician in private practice who is busy all day with her patients in addition to supervising her office staff. She wants to incorporate new time-management tools into her routine. She is unsure where to begin, and she has come to you for your advice.

1. **Paula wants to choose some helpful time-management tools, and she needs some help getting started. What should you tell her to do first?**

    a) Paula should delegate more of her work to her staff.

    b) Paula should reduce the number of activities she is participating in.

    c) Paula should ask other doctors for a critique of her work.

    d) Paula should make a list of the time-management tools discussed.

2. **As Paula considers the various time-management tools, what are some of the things she should do?**

    a) Paula should write down the ways that she imagines using the tool to her benefit.

    b) Paula should use all of the tools and decide after a few weeks which tools to keep using.

    c) Paula should list any potential drawbacks that she might encounter with a particular tool.

    d) Paula should ask friends and family for their advice on which tools she should use.

3. **True or False? The benefit of benchmarking is that Paula can take a shortcut by simply picking the time-management tools that were helpful to someone else.**

    ___ True

    ___ False

DISCOVERY ACTIVITY 4-6

Discussing Choosing Tools

Scenario:

Reflect on the following questions regarding choosing tools, and share your ideas during the group discussion.

1. Using the guidelines presented, analyze time-management tools and identify the tools you plan to use.

2. How do you think your personal work style, personality, preferences, and your type of job mesh with time-management tools?

3. Which of the recommended time-management tools have you used in the past? Which time-management tools have you found to best suit your preferences and work style? How have you used them to your advantage? Are there any tools that you've found to be ill-suited to your preferences and work style? In what ways did they prove ineffective for you, and why?

4. Which of the time-management tools identified did you choose to work with? How do you think these tools will change your approach to time management? Are there other tools you'd like to incorporate into your strategy?

5. Did you choose to reject any time-management tools because they don't match your preferences and style of working? If so, which did you reject? Were there any time-management tools that were new to you? Do you think you might like to try out these tools? Why or why not?

Lesson 4 Follow-up

In this lesson, you identified a collection of helpful tools that you can use to achieve better management of your time.

1. Consider the importance of negotiating for success as it relates to time management. How do you plan to use negotiation skills to your advantage in terms of improving your use of time?

2. Reflect on the ways that delegating tasks may be helpful to you. How do you expect to use delegating as part of your effort to improve your time-management skills?

LESSON 5
Creating an Action Plan

Lesson Objectives:

In this lesson, you will create an action plan for your time-management process and identify ways to evaluate and improve your efforts.

You will:

*   Create an action plan.
*   Evaluate the time-management process.

Lesson 5

Introduction

Effective time managers have a structured framework to guide their use of time. As they evaluate their progress, they refine their approach as needed so that they can continually make improvements. In this lesson, you will create an action plan to guide your time-management process and develop a system for evaluating and improving your efforts.

Creating your own action plan will help you to tailor a time-management system to your own needs, requirements, and style of working. By creating an action plan, you will be better equipped to move ahead effectively while focusing on the areas you need to improve and leveraging the personal strengths that you embody.

TOPIC A

Create the Action Plan

You need an action plan to provide you with a strategic framework for your time-management efforts. In this topic, you will create your own action plan for time management.

Creating an action plan will help you move forward in your quest for improved time management. You will create the template and structure for your time-management efforts, and you will use it as your framework for implementing change.

Action Plan

Definition:

An *action plan* is your written blueprint for behavior. It documents your time-management plans and the tools and techniques you'll use. In your action plan, you identify the specific time-management steps you'll take and the strategies you'll use to target your problem areas. The action plan also outlines how you will align your priorities with your activities. It is unique to you; it takes into account your energy allocation and daily energy flow, as well as your work style and preferences, personal strengths, and motivators. It may be very specific and carefully detailed, or it may be just a general outline of your ideas.

Example:

Robert, a teacher, struggled with addressing his priorities, including meeting the curriculum and spending time with each student. His action plan identified the techniques and tools he'd use and how he'd incorporate them into his routine. He planned to use benchmarking and prioritizing. He'd benchmark his principal's example to observe his effective habits, and noted when he planned to observe him. He wrote out a list of questions to ask about how he addressed his priorities.

The school dictated Robert's routine, so he had little flexibility to block out quiet chunks of time. But Robert found new ways to schedule in his priorities, which included spending time with students in small groups. He invited five students each day to eat lunch with him, so that each week he had lunch with all 25 students. His action plan also required him to use an electronic planner to schedule faculty meetings, parent conferences, and appointments.

Priorities

Definition:

Your *priorities* are the tasks that you define as critical, meaning that you must complete them, and valuable, meaning that they will help you further your goals. Effective time management requires you to schedule in time to address your priorities first, before attending to noncritical or unproductive tasks. It is a mistake to allow your days to be consumed by tasks that are not defined as priorities.

Example:

Barry, a retail store manager, spent the majority of his time on the phone with customers and vendors; he had trouble finding time for his priorities, which included training his staff to be excellent customer service representatives. Barry needed to schedule time each day to address his priorities first. He decided to schedule a sales meeting each morning with his staff before his store opened for business.

Priority Alignment

Effective time management requires a direct correlation between your time and energy expenditures and your priorities. *Priority alignment* is the act of making sure that you are spending your time and energy on your most important tasks, projects, and activities. It helps you ensure that you are managing your time well.

How to Create the Action Plan

By creating an effective action plan, you can specify exactly which time-management tools, techniques, and strategies you will use to improve your effective allocation of time and energy.

Guidelines

To create your action plan, follow these guidelines:

- Review the goals you've identified for yourself.
  - Are your goals realistic?
  - Have you identified both a short-term goal and a long-term goal?
  - Have you included a time frame for completion?
- Review the significant factors of your work life that affect your ability to use time effectively, such as your personal working style, your organizational preferences, your inherent strengths and attributes, and the internal and external factors that motivate you to be productive. You can use all of these factors to your advantage by adapting your work environment, schedule, and surroundings, as much as possible, to those that suit you best.
- Review the time-management tools, techniques, and strategies that are available. These include:
  - Diplomatic solutions or refusals
  - Interruption control
  - Appropriate delegation
  - Benchmarks
  - Time's monetary value
  - Calendars

— Electronic planners

— To-do lists

— Multitasking

— Deadlines

— Priorities

- Create a written action plan for yourself that identifies all of the strategies, tools, and techniques you intend to use.

  — Be as specific as possible.

  — Identify which tool you will use to address each time-management issue that you face.

- Summarize the behavioral changes that you intend to make. What do you intend to do differently in the coming days and weeks to manage your time more effectively?

- Include a projection of how you expect these behavioral changes to help you meet your goals.

- Include a time frame for your action plan. It can be one week or longer. At the end of the designated time frame, you will be ready to re-evaluate your action plan for effectiveness.

MY ACTION PLAN

My goals:
Short-term: To sign up for an entry-level accounting class this month.
Long-term: To pursue a management position.

The time-management tools I will use:
1) Diplomatic refusals to turn down the extra activities I don't want to take on.
2) Interruption control to save myself time during the workday.
3) Time's monetary value to remind myself of the value of each working hour.

My written action plan:
I am going to incorporate diplomatic refusals so that I can turn down some of the activities I don't want to take on and interruption control so that I can take control of my workday and avoid distractions from colleagues. I'll also use time's monetary value to remind myself of the value of my working hours.

My projection:
I think that by using these tools I can use my time better during the workday, become more effective on the job, and pursue the management position that I want. I think if I can take better control of my time I will become more productive. I need to utilize diplomatic refusals because one of my major time wasters is spending time chatting with friends during the workday.

My time frame:
I plan to evaluate my action plan at the end of three week and see how I am doing with implementing my new time-management tools. I may need to tweak my efforts after three weeks if these tools aren't effective enough.

Figure 5-1: *A sample action plan.*

Example:

Jack, an operations manager for a manufacturing firm, created an action plan. He reviewed his goals, which included reducing the number of workplace accidents by devoting more time to hands-on training of his staff. Then he reviewed his personal style. Jack is most effective as a trainer when he's energized by a group of people. His motivators include his job requirement to reduce accidents, his enjoyment of his management position, and his competitive streak.

Jack considered different tools and strategies. Since he had a tendency to try to take on too much, he decided to practice incorporating diplomatic refusals into his routine to diminish the number of requests he accepts. He also decided to start controlling interruptions, and began posting his daily schedule outside his office so the staff would know when he was available to talk. He posted his written action plan where he could see it.

Jack created a weekly calendar. For each workday, he charted the time-management behaviors he would use. He scheduled himself to be on the factory floor for three hours of intensive hands-on training every morning, and planned to be unavailable for impromptu calls and meetings during those hours. Jack's written projection stipulated that he would have his new time-management techniques incorporated into his routine within two weeks.

DISCOVERY ACTIVITY 5-1

Creating an Action Plan

Scenario:

Frank is a human resources assistant working for a payroll processing company. Frank's supervisor, Karen, relies on him to manage many different tasks during the course of a day and frequently gives him additional work. It's sometimes difficult for Frank to accommodate all of Karen's wishes and also attend to his routine assignments. Frank wants to create an action plan for his time-management efforts, but he's not sure how to get started. Frank has come to you asking for advice.

1. **Which of the following considerations are among those that Frank should keep in mind as he begins to create his action plan?**

    a) Frank should consider his goals.

    b) Frank should consider his personal strengths.

    c) Frank should consider Karen's energy level.

    d) Frank should consider Karen's work preferences.

2. As Frank creates his action plan, he needs to review the available time-management tools, techniques, and strategies. Which of the following are among those that Frank should consider?

   a) Frank should ask Karen to create an action plan for him.

   b) Instead of creating an action plan, Frank should consider working longer hours.

   c) Frank should consider benchmarking someone else's good example.

   d) An action plan probably won't help Frank, who needs to concentrate on his job.

3. True or False? A written action plan identifies all of the strategies, tools, and techniques you intend to use, and it summarizes the behavioral changes that you hope other people will make.

   ___ True

   ___ False

DISCOVERY ACTIVITY 5-2

Discussing the Action Plan

Scenario:

Reflect on the following questions regarding an action plan, and share your ideas during the group discussion.

1. Using the guidelines presented, create an action plan.

2. As you review the goals you have identified for yourself, are they realistic? What is your short-term goal? What is your long-term goal? What is your time frame for completion?

3. How did reviewing the goals you set for yourself influence your creation of an action plan? How did your goals dictate your action plan development?

4. How did your review of your personal style, motivators, personal strengths, and preferences influence your creation of your action plan? How did you incorporate these various elements into your plan? Were there other elements of your personal style that you wanted to incorporate into the plan, but you weren't sure how to do it? If so, how did you address those issues?

5. Now that you've summarized the behavioral changes you intend to make, how do you feel about moving forward? Do you think these behavioral changes will be difficult for you to implement on the job? Why or why not? How do you think having a written action plan will help to make it easier to implement behavioral changes?

TOPIC B

Evaluate the Time-Management Process

Time management is an ongoing process. Even with an action place in place, you may still need to evaluate your efforts to determine whether they are producing the results that you want, and then refine and refocus your efforts as necessary. In this topic, you will evaluate the time-management process so that you can make any necessary adjustments.

Evaluating your time-management process will help you determine whether or not your efforts are producing the results you want. You will become an even more effective time manager by assessing your efforts and making changes to your process as needed.

Criteria

Definition:

Criteria are the standards that provide a basis for comparison. Time-management criteria are the basic standards that will help you measure the effectiveness of your time-management efforts. You will judge your own efforts against standard criteria so that you can measure your performance and make any necessary corrections to improve your performance.

Use standard criteria for evaluation by asking yourself the following questions: Are you meeting your goals? Are you addressing your priorities? Are you effectively addressing valuable and critical tasks? You may also use additional criteria of your own choosing. For example, you may choose to weigh your feelings of satisfaction or dissatisfaction with your results, or evaluate whether you feel that you are controlling your time effectively enough.

Example:

Chris, a sales representative, evaluated her time-management action plan. She measured her efforts against standard criteria, asking herself whether she was meeting her goals, addressing her priorities, and effectively addressing valuable tasks. Chris was meeting her long-term goal of making her sales quotas, and meeting her priority of satisfying her customers' daily orders. She was also addressing her valuable tasks, which included calling on five new accounts each week. Her evaluation included these standard criteria.

But while Chris could see that her productivity had increased, she wasn't fully satisfied with her results. She felt she was still spending too much time on nuisance tasks, such as unproductive staff meetings and unnecessarily long meetings with management. Her action plan evaluation included not only standard criteria, but also her subjective opinion. Since Chris believed she could improve even further, she resolved to focus on those outstanding issues as she moved forward.

Issues and Causes

Definition:

As you move through the process of evaluating your efforts and weighing your results against standard criteria, you may identify outstanding areas of concern. *Issues* are the unresolved time-management problems that need further work. *Causes* are the underlying reasons for these outstanding time-management problems.

Time-management issues and causes are different for each person. They will depend on various factors, including your job situation, the unique demands on your time, and the way in which you interact with others. Your time-management issues will not come as a surprise to you; these are the problems that have been preventing you from achieving your greatest productivity all along. As you evaluate your time-management process, you will focus clearly on these issues and target their causes with new solutions.

Example:

Brian, a medical researcher, worked through the process of evaluating his time-management efforts. By applying objective criteria, he was able to determine that he was meeting his goals in three key areas: he'd recently begun submitting his reports on time, he was able to finish his lab work on schedule, and he'd made significant progress on his preparations for an upcoming conference.

But Brian also identified an outstanding issue. He had not yet resolved the problem of others wasting his time while he was at work. He had several colleagues who liked to spend part of each morning and afternoon socializing with him, and departmental meetings invariably dragged on with unnecessary chitchat. Brian resolved to try new solutions. He chose to use diplomatic refusals and interruption control to address these outstanding issues.

Creative Solutions

Targeting the causes of your outstanding issues will require creative solutions. If the tools, techniques, or strategies that you have employed so far have proved ineffective for you, then you need to tweak your action plan and try another approach.

For example, if you have been using calendars throughout your time-management process and you are still missing appointments, then you might consider a different tool, such as an electronic planner. If diplomatic solutions have not resolved your interpersonal issues, then try a different technique, such as interruption control. Time management is a fluid, continually changing process; if you are not seeing the desired results, you must try another approach. Refine and refocus your efforts as needed.

How to Evaluate the Time-Management Process

A good evaluation of your time-management work results in the identification of any outstanding issues alongside the strategies you will use to target them as you move forward.

Guidelines

To help you evaluate your time-management efforts, follow these guidelines:

- Review your action plan. Using the standard criteria for evaluation, scrutinize the effectiveness of your efforts. Answer these questions:
    - Are you meeting your goals?
    - Are you addressing your priorities?
    - Are you effectively addressing your valuable and critical tasks?

- Rate your effectiveness on a scale of 1 to 5, with 5 being the most effective. Summarize your results; note the specific ways in which you have become more productive at work as a result of your time-management efforts.

- If your rating is not a 5, then there is room for improvement. Identify the goals, priorities, or tasks that you have not yet been able to effectively address. These outstanding obstacles are your issues.

- Identify the underlying reasons for these issues. What factors have prevented you from achieving your stated goals? These underlying reasons are your causes.

- Now you have identified your outstanding time-management issues and their causes. Review the time-management tools, techniques, and strategies that are available. From these, choose additional or different solutions. You will use these to address your outstanding issues.

- Revise your action plan to incorporate your new solutions. Give yourself specific instructions so that you have a strategic framework for how you will move forward using these different or additional tools.

Example:

Anne, a forensic accountant, wanted to evaluate her time-management efforts. With her action plan in hand, she scrutinized her work. By objectively assessing her results, she realized that she had met some of her goals. Her productivity had improved; she had increased the number of cases she worked on, and she had reduced the amount of time spent completing each assignment.

But Anne had not met all of her goals. One of her job requirements was to begin mentoring junior accountants in her firm, and her original action plan had not effectively addressed this critical but time-consuming priority. This was her outstanding time-management issue. She had to revise her action plan, choosing a new strategy.

Anne reviewed the time-management tools, strategies, and techniques, and decided to use a combination of them. She decided to use diplomatic solutions to negotiate with management regarding the number of people she was expected to mentor. And she would use multitasking to mentor three people simultaneously in group sessions, instead of working with them individually. Anne revised her action plan, incorporating these new solutions.

DISCOVERY ACTIVITY 5-3

Evaluating the Time-Management Process

Scenario:

Naomi, a recruitment officer, has been working through the time-management process, and she wants to evaluate her progress, measure how she's done so far, and see whether she needs to make any changes to improve further. Naomi feels that certain parts of her efforts are going quite well, but she may need improvement in some areas. She has come to you asking for your advice in evaluating her work.

1. **Naomi needs to begin evaluating her progress. What is the first question she should ask herself?**

   a) Naomi should ask herself why she hasn't yet met all of her goals and priorities.

   b) Naomi should ask herself how she can work more quickly.

   c) Naomi should ask herself who she can appropriately delegate projects to.

   d) Naomi should ask herself whether she has met her goals.

2. **If Naomi decides that she has effectively met her goals and addressed her priorities and her critical and valuable tasks, then what are the next steps she should take?**

   a) Naomi should rate her time-management effectiveness on a scale of 1 to 5.

   b) Naomi should ask others for their advice in moving forward productively.

   c) Naomi should summarize her results, noting how she has become more productive at work.

   d) Naomi should curtail her efforts at managing her time.

3. **True or False? If Naomi has effectively evaluated her time-management work, she will have identified any outstanding issues as well as the strategies she will use to address them.**

   ___ True

   ___ False

DISCOVERY ACTIVITY 5-4

Discussing Results

Scenario:

Reflect on the following questions regarding an action plan, and share your ideas during the group discussion.

1. Using the guidelines presented, evaluate your time-management process.

2. As you worked on your action plan, were you pleased with your results? What part of your action plan do you think you will find most helpful, and why?

3. What do you think your stumbling blocks will be as you implement your action plan? Are these stumbling blocks the same issues that you have struggled with in the past?

4. Do you think it will be difficult for you to implement new or different time-management strategies into your routine? Why or why not? Do you think that any of your outstanding time-management problems are intractable? If so, how do you intend to move forward effectively?

Lesson 5 Follow-up

In this lesson, you created an action plan for time management and identified ways to evaluate and improve your efforts.

1. Consider the importance of creating an action plan. How do you think this will improve your use of time and energy?

2. Reflect on the ways that you can evaluate your efforts. How do you anticipate using self-evaluation to your advantage as you move forward?

Follow-up

In this course, you identified some of the effective time-management strategies that will help you gain control of your time and accomplish more of your goals. You defined your personal and professional goals, established your priorities, and identified the critical tasks that you need to focus on. You also created a personal time-management action plan to guide your efforts moving forward.

1. Reflect on the importance of identifying time-management strategies and tools that work for you. How do you intend to use this newfound knowledge to your advantage on the job?

2. Consider the need to reduce time wasters, align activities with priorities, and leverage your strengths in the workplace. How will this enhance your own philosophy of time management?

3. Think about all the ways that you can incorporate time-management tools into your routine. How will this influence your behavior as you move forward?

What's Next?

Continue to evaluate your progress. After a month of implementation, re-evaluate your efforts on your time-management action plan, and refocus or refine your efforts as necessary.

LESSON LABS

Due to classroom setup constraints, some labs cannot be keyed in sequence immediately following their associated lesson. Your instructor will tell you whether your labs can be practiced immediately following the lesson or whether they require separate setup from the main lesson content.

LESSON 1 LAB 1

Understanding Goals

Scenario:

Janrex is an international corporation with offices in San Jose, New York City, London, Tokyo, and Helsinki that offers a wide variety of goods and services. In the upcoming quarter, Janrex will pursue a competitive bid for a major new account, and the company needs its employees to increase their productivity in order to win this business. The company has asked you to serve as a consultant. You will be asked to help a key employee improve her time-management skills so that her productivity can increase.

1. In order to participate in an interactive business simulation, launch the business simulation executable file for this lesson on the CD-ROM.

LESSON 2 LAB 1

Analyzing Energy and Time

Objective:

In this activity, you will explore your actual use of time and energy by keeping an extended time log.

LESSON LABS

Scenario:

You can compile meaningful objective data about your actual usage of time and energy if you keep a time log for an extended period, such as one standard work week. During this week, document your use of time and energy with as much detail as possible. Your time log will yield even more helpful data if you include non-working hours. Begin the time log when you wake in the morning, and keep documenting your time and energy until you retire at night. The more detail you include on your time log, the more meaningful and instructive data it will yield.

1. **At the beginning of your time log, write down your perceptions about how you use your time and energy.** How effective and productive do you imagine yourself to be? How many hours each day do you imagine that you devote to tasks that actually further your goals? How many hours each day do you imagine that you devote to activities that are neither critical, nor valuable, nor enjoyable?

2. **Throughout each day, make notes on your time log as frequently as possible. When you take a call from a colleague, for example, jot down the time at the beginning and the end of the call. Make notes to yourself.** Strive to develop a heightened awareness of how you actually use your time and energy. How much time during that call was spent discussing work-related topics? How much time was spent on non-work conversation?

3. As you reflect on the week, you may choose to make value judgments about the choices that you made about using your time and energy. Looking back, were there any periods that you would objectively classify as wasted time because you did not pursue valuable, critical, or enjoyable activities? For example, if you spent five hours watching television that you didn't find enjoyable, interesting, or relaxing, you might decide that those hours were wasted, and you might choose to make different choices next week. Were there any choices that you made during your extended time log period that you would like to approach differently in the future? **Take notes on your reflections.**

4. **At the end of the extended time log, review your data.** Can you notice any patterns in your energy cycle? Do you notice any times of the day in which you are consistently productive and energetic? Do you notice any times of the day in which your energy and productivity diminish?

5. **Return to the beginning of the time log and review the projections you made at the beginning of the week. Summarize your results.** How did your actual use of time and energy during this period compare to your perception? Does your data show that you used your time and energy more effectively or less effectively than you imagined? Were there any surprises for you in how you actually spend your time and energy? As you review your data, what conclusions can you draw about your use of time and energy?

LESSON 3 LAB 1

Describing Your Personal Style

Objective:

In this activity, you will write a letter to a fellow time-management practitioner, analyzing your personal style.

Scenario:

As you reflect on your personal style, you can summarize some of the highlights that make you unique and contribute to your effective use of time and energy. Summarize your reflections by writing an expert letter to anther person who is struggling with the time-management process. In this letter, you will share the benefit of your experience with the time-management process. You will describe yourself, your world view, your strengths and preferences, your motivators, and even your time wasters and explain how these factors affect time management.

1. **In your letter, describe your successful past project or event. Tell your fellow time manager in detail about what you accomplished and how you were effective.** What were the strategies you used? What were the results of your efforts? What are some of the time-management tips and tricks you used that you want to share?

2. **Tell the other time manager about your own world view and your work style, and how these elements contribute to your philosophy about time and energy usage.** What is there about your use of time that's uniquely effective? What can you share about your work preferences and your style? In what ways do you think your style works to your advantage? In what ways do you think your style might hinder your effectiveness?

3. **In your letter, describe your personal strengths. Share any details in your letter that might be relevant or instructive to another person who is working on time-management issues.** What are your strengths? How do you use them to your advantage in the workplace? How do your strengths contribute to your use of time?

4. **Tell the other time manager what your motivators are. Describe both internal and external motivators.** How do you leverage these motivators to your advantage on the job? What ideas can you share about keeping yourself motivated?

5. **Share some of your problematic time wasters with the other time manager, as well as your ideas for reducing them.** What are the time wasters that you struggle with the most? What are the time wasters that you have effectively overcome? What strategies have you developed to effectively deal with other people who waste your time?

LESSON 4 LAB 1

Understanding Time-Management Tools

Scenario:

Janrex is an international corporation with offices in San Jose, New York City, London, Tokyo, and Helsinki that offers a wide variety of goods and services. Robert Schwartz is a valued, long-term client of Janrex goods and services. Robert has just approached the Janrex management team with a new request. Due to new government accounting regulations, an upcoming IRS audit, and some accounting irregularities, Robert needs Janrex to investigate some issues and produce detailed documentation for his company's business activity for the past three years.

1. In order to participate in an interactive business simulation, launch the business simulation executable file for this lesson on the CD-ROM.

LESSON 5 LAB 1

Defending the Action Plan

Objective:

In this activity, you will prepare to defend your action plan in front of a panel of experts at a time-management conference.

Scenario:

You have been invited to present your action plan to a panel of experts at a time-management conference. If they are impressed with your work, they may consider publishing your action plan in a new textbook on time management. You will present your action plan and then field questions from the experts about how you created it, what it includes, and how you will measure its effectiveness. You can expect that they will thoroughly scrutinize your work, and you will be expected to defend the choices you have made throughout the process of developing your action plan. Write out an outline of the points you will present at the conference, and prepare in advance to answer the questions the experts are likely to ask you.

1. **Consider how you will explain to the experts what an action plan is. You may want to describe the underlying philosophy behind creating an action plan.** How is an action plan designed to contribute to a person's overall time-management process?

2. You will want to share the main elements of your action plan with the experts. **Explain how it responds to your defined priorities. Describe how it reflects your work style and preferences, and how it summarizes the behavioral changes you intend to make.**

3. The panel of experts will want to know how an action plan incorporates time-management strategies, tools, and techniques. **Consider how you will explain how you incorporated strategies and tools into your action plan. You will also want to describe the results of your action plan and how you will use it to guide your behavior moving forward.**

4. The experts will ask you how you can measure the effectiveness of your action plan. **You will want to describe the process of evaluating an action plan. Describe in detail what the evaluation encompasses, and then describe how you will revise and refine the plan once you have completed your evaluation.**

NOTES

SOLUTIONS

Lesson 1

Activity 1-1

1. Leah knows that she needs to improve her use of time. What is the first step for Leah?

   ✓ a) Defining what it is that she hopes to accomplish.

   b) Identifying how she likes to work.

   c) Identifying her personal strengths.

   d) Creating an action plan for time management.

2. Leah must be a competent person, since she has managed to become a published cookbook author. Why should she waste more time on time management, when she could just spend her time working harder?

   ✓ a) Leah is already working hard, but she is not necessarily working effectively.

   b) Leah is not a competent person, as evidenced by her failure to get her work done each day.

   c) Leah's time-management problems would be solved if she had an office outside of her home.

   d) Leah has the same problem that many working mothers have, and there is no solution until the children are grown.

Activity 1-2

1. What do you think of the time-management process as it was defined? How does this change or influence your understanding of time management?

   Answers will vary.

2. How do you anticipate that your time-management process will be influenced by thinking about your dreams for the future? In what ways do you think this will guide your efforts?

   Answers will vary.

3. What are some of the everyday problems that you have with your time management? What are some of the things you hope to do differently as a result of working through this process?

   Answers will vary.

SOLUTIONS

Activity 1-3

1. If Deborah is having trouble getting started, how should she begin describing her dreams?

    a) She should make a comprehensive list of everything she wants to do.

    b) She should postpone describing her dreams until she finds some free time.

    c) She should focus on the obstacles standing in her way.

    ✓ d) She should identify one small dream.

2. Ideally, the dreams that Deborah identifies should have certain characteristics. Which of these are among them?

    a) Deborah's dreams should relate to what she hopes her employer will offer her.

    b) Deborah's dreams should be fantastic and "pie in the sky."

    ✓ c) Deborah's dreams can be large or small as long as they are within the realm of possibility.

    ✓ d) Deborah should identify what she'd like to improve or develop in her personal life.

Activity 1-4

1. What are some of the big achievements you'd like to make? How do you think it would benefit you or your family if you achieved them? What are some of the milestones you'd like to reach in your career?

Answers will vary.

2. What are some of the small improvements you'd like to make? What are some habits you think you might like to change? Are there any small dreams that you think you could achieve within the next six months?

Answers will vary.

3. Have you ever considered time-management within the context of dreams before? How do you think reflecting on your dreams for the future will influence your efforts to manage your time?

Answers will vary.

4. Once you've given some thought to focusing on your dreams, do you think this will change how you think about using time as a resource? Why or why not? Do you think that keeping your mind on what you hope to accomplish over the long term can help you use your time well today?

Answers will vary.

5. Is this the first time in your professional life that you've thought carefully about your dreams for the future? Do you find it easy or difficult to think about time management within the context of long-term planning? Are you a person who enjoys planning for the future, or do you prefer to focus on today?

Answers will vary.

Activity 1-5

1. Jackson wants to describe his regrets. What should he consider?

   a) He should consider past events that were beyond his control.

   b) He should consider past events that had little bearing on his life.

   c) He should consider the regrets of other people around him.

   ✓ d) He should consider choices he's made that have had repercussions for his life.

2. Jackson has many regrets. Which of the following are among the regrets that Jackson should consider relevant for the purposes of improving his time management?

   ✓ a) Jackson's professional regret is that he doesn't have the MBA that would help him pursue management positions.

   ✓ b) Jackson's big regret is that he allowed himself to run up significant debt many years ago.

   c) Jackson's personal regret is that he never had the son he always wanted.

   ✓ d) Jackson's small regret is that he never keeps his New Year's resolution to lose 10 pounds.

Activity 1-6

1. What is something that you wish you had done, or not done, in your professional life in the past? How has this awareness of a past professional regret informed the choices that you make on the job now?

   Answers will vary.

2. Is there a regret that you identified that causes you minor annoyance and irritation? How will the awareness of this minor regret change or influence your behavior moving forward?

   Answers will vary.

3. What do you think about using your regrets about the past as part of the basis for thinking about using time effectively? Do you think this will be helpful to you? Why or why not?

   Answers will vary.

4. In this topic, we reviewed guidelines for identifying regrets. What did you discover about your regrets as a result of this process? Were there any surprises for you?

   Answers will vary.

5. In your professional life, have you given thought to regrets before, or are you more focused on the future? How do you think it might help you to manage your time better if you think about your regrets? What part of this topic did you find most helpful as you think about making better time-management choices?

   Answers will vary.

SOLUTIONS

Activity 1-7

1. C.J. has defined her goals this way: "I always wanted to be a nurse. I would like to go back to school someday for some kind of nursing job." Is this a good description of C.J.'s goals?

   a) No, because she has not investigated whether there are nursing jobs available in her area.

   b) Yes, this is an excellent description of C.J.'s goals.

   ✓ c) No, because C.J. has not included a proposed timeline or specific behavior that she expects of herself.

   d) No, because a good description of goals includes what she hopes other people will do for her.

2. C.J. needs to know whether she has appropriately described her goals. Which of the following accurately reflects a well-articulated goal?

   ✓ a) A good description of your goals clearly outlines what you expect of yourself.

   b) A well-articulated goal is a private hope that you probably will never achieve.

   c) A well-articulated goal implies that you know exactly how you will achieve it.

   d) A well-articulated goal is the same thing as a dream.

3. Why should C.J. spend time articulating her goals, when she can't even get her daily schedule under control?

   ✓ a) Articulating her goals will help C.J. strategize her time and energy allocation.

   b) C.J. will feel better about herself if she articulates her goals.

   c) C.J. needs to articulate her goals before she can choose a new, less stressful job or career path.

   d) Articulating her goals will give C.J. a welcome break from her office routine.

Activity 1-8

1. Which dreams and regrets did you use as the basis for forming your goals? Can you describe one of the goals you have established for yourself?

   Answers will vary.

2. Your goals should be challenging but achievable. What are some of the elements of your goals that will make them challenging for you? What factors have led you to conclude that your goals are also achievable?

   Answers will vary.

3. Have you given much thought to your goals in the past? How effective have you been in meeting some of your goals?

   Answers will vary.

4. Do you see any connection between your goals and how you choose to use your time today? How do you think your goals will influence how you use your time? Have you struggled with achieving goals in the past? How important do you think time management is in terms of pursuing your goals?

   Answers will vary.

5. Do you think it's challenging to focus on goals for the future when each daily routine is perhaps very full? How do you think that focusing on your goals might change the way you approach each day?

    Answers will vary.

Lesson 2

Activity 2-1

1. Roger is keeping a time log in his office. At the end of the day today, he plans to jot down all of the activities he remembers. Which of the following is an accurate statement about Roger's time log?

    a) Roger is completing the time log in accordance with the instructions.

    ✓ b) Roger needs to work on and revise the time log throughout the day.

    c) Roger won't benefit from keeping a time log until he gets his schedule under control.

    d) Roger should complete his time log on his day off, when he has free time.

2. Which of the following statements about Roger's time log is true?

    a) To save time, Roger can take good mental notes about his activities and fill in his time log later.

    ✓ b) Roger should include distractions and interruptions on his time log.

    c) Roger should only include productive activities on his time log.

    d) Roger should only include work-related activities on his time log.

3. True or False? Roger should draw a check mark on his time log to highlight periods of productivity.

    ___ True

    _✓_ False

Activity 2-2

1. How do you think you might benefit from keeping a time log? Have you ever tried to track your time in the past? How do you think this exercise will influence your use of time?

    Answers will vary.

2. Note the sample time log shown. How closely does this time log follow the recommended guidelines? Does the sample time log in any way fail to follow the recommended guidelines? How effective do you think this sample time log will be to the person who completed it? How could this person improve the time log? Please explain.

    Answers will vary.

Solutions

Activity 2-3

1. What are some of your personal tasks? What are some of your professional tasks? What are some of your recreational tasks?

   Answers will vary.

2. Which of your tasks have been assigned to you by others? Which of your tasks have you chosen for yourself? Which of your tasks do you find enjoyable?

   Answers will vary.

Activity 2-4

1. Karen has compiled a list of her daily tasks and now she wants to analyze them. What else does she need?

   a) Karen needs her principal's input.

   b) Karen needs to consult with other teachers.

   c) Karen has everything she needs.

   ✓ d) Karen needs to consult her time log.

2. How should Karen mark the tasks on her task list that are neither valuable, nor critical, nor enjoyable?

   a) Karen should mark them with a "V".

   b) Karen should mark them with an "E".

   c) Karen should cross them out.

   ✓ d) Karen should double-underline them.

3. True or False? Karen needs to analyze her current tasks. After Karen compiles a list of the tasks that consume her time, her next step should be reviewing her task list.

   ___ True

   ✓ False

Activity 2-5

1. Using the guidelines presented, create a time log. Using your time log to guide you, answer the following questions.

   Finished time logs will vary for each person.

2. What kinds of tasks consume your time on a typical day? When you developed your time log, do you think you were able to accurately report the time that you spent on activities?

   Answers will vary.

3. Which of your activities were critical? Which were valuable? Which were enjoyable? Did any of your activities fail to meet one of these categories? If so, do you think you might consider curtailing this activity in the future? Why or why not?

   Answers will vary.

4. What do you think about analyzing your tasks in terms of their value? Have you thought about evaluating your activities in this way before? How will this affect your energy allocation?

Answers will vary.

5. Have you encountered the 80/20 rule before? How does it influence how you will assess your allocation of time and energy? Do you find yourself spending the bulk of your available resources on nonessential tasks? How can the 80/20 rule help you to spend your time and energy more wisely?

Answers will vary.

6. How adept are you at time estimation? Can you think of an instance when estimating your time accurately proved to be a valuable skill? If you have difficulty estimating the time needed for various tasks, how do you think you can use the information here to improve?

Answers will vary.

Activity 2-6

1. Sheila wants to analyze her time usage. She needs to identify how her time is wasted. Which activities are likely to be her most problematic time wasters?

   a) Activities that are critical.

   ✓ b) Activities that have high cost and low benefits and are neither valuable, critical, nor enjoyable.

   c) Activities that are enjoyable but low cost.

   d) Activities that are valuable only to Sheila.

2. If Sheila wants to analyze her time usage, what does she need to have readily available?

   ✓ a) Her cost-benefit chart

   b) An itemized list of her vacation days from the last year

   c) A spreadsheet of her time for the last year

   d) A clock or watch

3. True or False? Activities that are high cost, low benefit, and not valuable, not critical, and not enjoyable are most likely time wasters.

   ✓ True

   ___ False

Activity 2-7

1. Using the guidelines presented, analyze your time usage.

   Time usage will vary for each person.

2. When you analyzed your time usage, which of your activities did you find to have the greatest cost and the greatest benefit? Which of your activities have the greatest cost and the lowest benefit? Were there any surprises for you when you analyzed your time usage?

   Answers will vary.

3. What were some of the premier time wasters that you identified? Did any of these surprise you? Were you previously aware that these activities are unproductive? Do you think you might consider curtailing these activities in the future? Why or why not?

   Answers will vary.

4. What are some of the sources of distraction in your life? How have you tried to address them?

   Answers will vary.

5. What is your opinion of the guidelines for analyzing your current time usage? Was it interesting and helpful to you to find out how you are spending your time?

   Answers will vary.

6. Based on the exercise of analyzing your time usage, what changes do you think you might make in your behavior? What did you learn or observe about your use of time that surprised you?

   Answers will vary.

Activity 2-8

1. Rhonda wants to analyze her energy flow. How should she begin?

   a) Rhonda should first focus on getting more sleep.

   b) Rhonda should ask other bank managers how they manage their time.

   ✓ c) Rhonda should first make a list of her personal energy sources.

   d) Rhonda should focus on her critical activities and not worry about her lack of energy.

2. When analyzing energy flow, what does Rhonda need to refer to on her time log?

   ✓ a) Rhonda needs to refer to the starred tasks.

   b) Rhonda needs to refer to the critical tasks.

   c) Rhonda needs to refer to the enjoyable tasks.

   d) Rhonda needs to refer to the underlined tasks.

3. True or False? The final step in analyzing your energy flow is writing down your most significant personal energy sources.

   ___ True

   _✓_ False

Activity 2-9

1. Using the guidelines presented, analyze your energy flow.

   Energy flow analysis will vary for each person.

2. What are some of your most significant personal energy sources? What are the times of the day when you are more energetic and productive?

   Answers will vary.

3. What are some of the highlights of your personal energy cycle? Have you ever tried to capitalize on these productive times in the past? How effective do you think you are at leveraging your most productive daily time periods?

Answers will vary.

4. What is your opinion of the guidelines for analyzing your energy flow? Did you find these guidelines instructive and helpful? Why or why not?

Answers will vary.

5. What kinds of experience have you had with momentum and burnout? Do you find these factors to be influential in your life? How do you like to capitalize on your momentum? How do you minimize the effects of burnout?

Answers will vary.

6. How do your personal energy sources help you function effectively? Are there additional sources of energy that you could be using? In your opinion, do highly effective people have more personal energy sources than less effective people?

Answers will vary.

Lesson 3

Activity 3-1

1. Lauren has come to you asking for your advice as she reflects on a past success. Which of the following would be among the steps she should take as she reflects on a past success?

    a) She should consider a career path that suits her better.

    b) She should make a list of the things she's failed to accomplish.

    ✓ c) She should consider the preparations that she made in advance of her past successful event.

    d) She should make a list of the things she'd like to accomplish in the future.

2. As Lauren reflects on a past successful day or event, which of the following are among the considerations she should include?

    ✓ a) Lauren should consider why that past success was important to her.

    ✓ b) Lauren should consider how that past event contributed to her goals.

    ✓ c) Lauren should consider the feedback she received from others.

    d) Lauren should consider what she should have done differently at that time.

3. True or False? In thinking about her past success, Lauren has chosen to describe "a day off, with nothing at all on the agenda." This is an appropriate choice within the context of reflecting on a past success.

    ___ True

    ✓ False

Activity 3-2

1. Using the guidelines presented, reflect on a past success.

   Past successes will vary for each person.

2. What was the past success that you chose to reflect on? What were some of the elements that led to your success? What were some of the special steps that you took to ensure success in that instance? What were some of the challenges you faced at that time, and how did you overcome them?

   Answers will vary.

3. Prior to taking this course, have you spent time considering your past successes? How helpful did you find this exercise? How does reflecting on your past successes influence your thinking? Does it change how you will approach future challenges?

   Answers will vary.

4. As you consider a past success, think about your effectiveness at replicating that success. What elements of that event have you been able to repeat? What elements of that successful event would you like to incorporate into your work life right now? How do you think that reflecting on past successful projects might boost your confidence or help you improve your productivity?

   Answers will vary.

5. Is this your first experience with incorporating past successes into efforts at improved time management? How do you intend to use your past successes to your advantage in approaching time management? Conversely, do you think it might help you in your time-management efforts if you reflect on some of your past projects that were not very successful? Why or why not?

   Answers will vary.

Activity 3-3

1. Ann wants to analyze her personal work preferences. What should she do first?

   ✓ a) Analyze her preferences by working through the recommended questions.

   b) Write a two-sentence description of her work style and preferences.

   c) Try to be more outgoing on the job.

   d) Put a Do Not Disturb sign on her office door each day.

2. Ann has come to you asking for your help as she tries to analyze her work preferences. Which of the following is among the recommended questions that you would suggest she try to answer?

   ✓ a) Do you feel most energized and productive working alone or in a group?

   ✓ b) Do you prefer to work closely with one or more teammates?

   ✓ c) Do you like to work steadily on one task at a time, or do you prefer to juggle several tasks at once?

   d) What do you believe is the most successful way to work?

Activity 3-4

1. Using the guidelines presented, analyze your work style preferences.

    Work style preferences will vary for each person.

2. As you analyzed your work style preferences, what were some of the things you discovered about yourself? In what circumstances do you feel most energetic, productive, and enthusiastic about work? Do you prefer to work independently or collaboratively?

    Answers will vary.

3. What are some of the elements of your work life that you would like to leverage more effectively? What would your ideal work space look, sound, and feel like? What would be the structure of your ideal workday?

    Answers will vary.

4. As you reflect on your preferences, what have you learned about your work style? How do you plan to try to incorporate more of your preferences into your working life? How do you think that leveraging your preferences might make you more effective at work?

    Answers will vary.

5. What are some of the work preferences you have that you have not yet found a way to incorporate into your current working life? Have you considered discussing with your supervisor some ideas for adapting your work environment to leverage your preferences? Why or why not?

    Answers will vary.

6. Which of your work preferences are you already leveraging to your advantage? What suggestions would you make to another student of time management about how you've incorporated your preferences into your work life? What ideas have you had that have helped you become more productive using your preferences?

    Answers will vary.

Activity 3-5

1. Donna has come to you to ask for help in creating her list of personal strengths. How would you advise her to begin?

    ✓ a) Tell Donna to make a comprehensive list of her qualities and attributes.

    b) Tell Donna to make a comprehensive list of the qualities and attributes she most admires in others.

    c) Tell Donna to review her résumé and identify the positions she has most enjoyed.

    d) Tell Donna to ask her supervisor for positive feedback.

2. Which of the following are among the recommended strategies for developing a good description of your personal strengths?

   ✓ a) You should include the assets that others have praised you for in the past.

   ✓ b) You should include the abilities that have helped you in your professional life.

   c) You should include the skills and abilities that you would like to develop in the future.

   ✓ d) You should include the assets and abilities that you have not yet put to use in the workplace.

3. True or False? When developing your list of personal strengths, it's appropriate to include the qualities that contribute to your social life, even if they do not relate to your current job.

   ✓ True

   ___ False

Activity 3-6

1. Using the guidelines presented, identify your strengths.

   Strengths will vary for each person.

2. What are some of the personal qualities and attributes that you identified? What are some of the skills, assets, and abilities that you have used in your professional life or during your education?

   Answers will vary.

3. What are some of the personal strengths you identified that you have not yet had a chance to use in the workplace? Can you think of ways that you might be able to incorporate them into your working life?

   Answers will vary.

4. What are some of the personal strengths that you have used to your advantage in the workplace? How have you effectively leveraged your strengths?

   Answers will vary.

5. Can you think of any strengths that you have developed over time? Are there any strengths that didn't come naturally to you, but that you've worked hard to incorporate into your life? Are there any strengths that you are using in your current position that you hadn't had a chance to use in the past?

   Answers will vary.

6. What are some of your hidden strengths? What are some of the qualities that you embody that you wish you could use more effectively in your working life? Do you have ideas for new ways that you could start leveraging your strengths more effectively on the job?

   Answers will vary.

Activity 3-7

1. Grant has asked you to help him identify some of his personal motivators. What would you ask him to do first?

   a) You would ask him to stop wasting his time during the work day.

   b) You would ask him to put a motivational sign near his desk that will remind him to keep working.

   ✓ c) You would ask him to make a list of all the personal motivators that he can think of.

   d) You would ask him to ask some more experienced salespeople for their advice.

2. Which of the following are among the steps that Grant should take to identify his personal motivators?

   ✓ a) He should list the positive influences that provide him with incentive.

   ✓ b) He should list any internal factors that give him motivation.

   c) He should list the influences that have provided motivation to famous people throughout history.

   ✓ d) He should list the emotional factors that provide him with incentive.

3. True or False? Personal motivators can be any factors that provide you with the drive and incentive to act.

   ✓ True

   __ False

Activity 3-8

1. Using the guidelines presented, identify your personal motivators.

   Motivators will vary for each person.

2. What are some of the personal motivators you identified? What are some of the positive factors that motivate you? What are some of the negative factors that motivate you?

   Answers will vary.

3. What are some of the personal motivators that have served you well throughout your working life? Have you ever had to try to find new sources of motivation on the job?

   Answers will vary.

4. What are some of the positive factors that provide you with incentive? What are some of the negative factors? Have you ever tried to come up with additional incentives to keep yourself motivated? How successful have you been in leveraging your motivators to your advantage?

   Answers will vary.

5. What are your motivators for improving your time-management process? Are your motivators powerful enough to change your behavior, or do you need to find additional motivational factors? Are there people in your working life who provide you with motivation on the job? Do you rely on other people to provide motivation, or are your motivating factors internal?

   Answers will vary.

SOLUTIONS

Activity 3-9

1. Danielle needs to find effective strategies for reducing time wasters, and she has come to you asking for your advice. What would you tell her to do first?

   a) Tell Danielle to ask everyone to leave her alone during the work day.

   b) Tell Danielle to make a to-do list each morning and accomplish everything on it.

   ✓ c) Tell Danielle to review her list of personal motivators.

   d) Tell Danielle to focus first on her work, and then focus on her personal life in her spare time.

2. Which of the following are among the recommended strategies that Danielle could consider?

   ✓ a) Danielle could consider enlisting the help of her coworkers and supervisors.

   ✓ b) Danielle could consider developing polite responses to interruptions.

   c) Danielle could consider taking a demotion so that she has a more manageable job.

   ✓ d) Danielle could consider chunking similar tasks together.

3. True or False? For each problematic time waster, there is one specific strategy that should work for everyone.

   ___ True

   _✓_ False

Activity 3-10

1. Using the guidelines presented, identify your troublesome time wasters.

   Time wasters will vary for each person.

2. What are some of the troublesome time wasters that you identified? What are some of the strategies you have decided to use to address your time wasters?

   Answers will vary.

3. Have you tried to address your time wasters in the past? If so, what strategies did you use? How successful have you been?

   Answers will vary.

4. Sometimes, our most difficult time wasters are those caused by other people. How have you tried to address time-wasting issues caused by others? How did the other people respond to you? If your experience was less than satisfactory, how would you approach this differently in the future?

   Answers will vary.

5. For some people, reducing time wasters at work is a new prospect. Had you ever tried to actively reduce your time wasters before? What are some of the strategies that you've found most effective? What are some of the strategies that you plan to try for the first time?

   Answers will vary.

Effective Time Management

Lesson 4

Activity 4-1

1. Larry has come to you for advice regarding some of the negotiating tools that he wants to develop. What would you suggest that Larry should do first?

    a) Larry should begin by refusing all new requests for help.

    b) Larry should begin by closing the door of his office each day until all his work is done.

    ✓ c) Larry should begin by making a list of his most frequent time-management problems.

    d) Larry should begin reminding Dana that he's well-liked by the staff and his heart is in the right place.

2. Larry is weighing his options. Which of the following techniques are part of the recommended strategy for negotiating time-management success as they have been defined here?

    ✓ a) Larry should first list his frequent time-management issues.

    ✓ b) Larry should write down some possible strategies for addressing his identified time-management issues.

    c) Larry should ask his colleagues for their helpful suggestions.

    d) Larry should research time-management strategies on the Internet.

3. True or False? If Larry is uncomfortable refusing extra activities that he doesn't have time for, then he should simply agree to do them anyway.

    ___ True

    _✓_ False

Activity 4-2

1. Using the guidelines presented, identify helpful negotiating strategies.

    Negotiating strategies will vary for each person.

2. What are some of the most problematic time-management problems that you face regularly? Have you tried to address them in the past? If so, what kinds of strategies have you tried? Are there any effective and unique strategies that you've developed that you can share?

    Answers will vary.

3. What ideas have you had for incorporating diplomatic refusals on the job? Have you tried using diplomatic refusals? If so, how did people respond to you? Were you surprised if people responded well to your polite refusal or negotiation? How does the concept of diplomatic refusals influence your thinking about taking control of your own time?

    Answers will vary.

4. Negotiating skills are a new behavior for some people. Are you developing negotiating skills for the first time? Does effective negotiation come easily to you, or do you have to work at it? What are some of the considerations that you like to keep in mind whenever you enter a negotiation with another person? Have you developed helpful ideas about negotiating skills that you can share with others?

Answers will vary.

Activity 4-3

1. Zachary has come to you asking for your advice on how to select tasks that would be appropriate to delegate to others. What would you tell him to do first?

    a) Zachary should first accomplish the most important tasks himself, and then delegate the less important tasks to others.

    b) Zachary should first find volunteers who can help him with some of the work.

    c) Zachary should first ask the people on his staff which tasks they would like to take over.

    ✓ d) Zachary should first make a list of his tasks and responsibilities.

2. One of the responsibilities that Zachary might consider delegating is the training of volunteers. As he considers this option, what are some of the questions he should ask himself?

    ✓ a) Can someone else take responsibility for this task, or do I need to do it myself?

    ✓ b) Do I have the authority to delegate this task to someone else?

    c) Is there anyone who would enjoy taking over this task?

    d) If I work longer hours, is it possible that I can complete this task myself?

3. True or False? Before Zachary delegates a task to someone else, he should consider whether he'll need to supervise the other person's performance.

    ✓ True

    ___ False

Activity 4-4

1. Using the guidelines presented, analyze your tasks to decide which tasks you can appropriately delegate.

    Task analysis will vary for each person.

2. What are some of the tasks you are currently responsible for? Are any of them specifically entrusted to you by your employer? Do you have the authority to delegate any tasks?

    Answers will vary.

3. Have you tried delegating some of your tasks in the past? What have your experiences with delegating been like? Have you ever found that your attempt to delegate a task has met with resistance from the other person? How did you resolve that issue?

    Answers will vary.

4. Had you ever before given conscious thought to appropriate versus inappropriate delegation? How do the recommended guidelines for judging appropriateness align with your experience? Have you ever had another person try to delegate tasks to you inappropriately? How did you respond? Why do you think it's necessary to have the authority to delegate a task? In your experience, what happens when people delegate tasks without authority?

    Answers will vary.

5. Have you ever made a choice to train another person to take over a task for you? If so, did you consider this a form of delegation? In the final analysis, was it an effective time-saving step for you to take? How did the upfront investment in training time compare to the eventual benefit of handing off the task to someone else?

    Answers will vary.

Activity 4-5

1. Paula wants to choose some helpful time-management tools, and she needs some help getting started. What should you tell her to do first?

    a) Paula should delegate more of her work to her staff.

    b) Paula should reduce the number of activities she is participating in.

    c) Paula should ask other doctors for a critique of her work.

    ✓ d) Paula should make a list of the time-management tools discussed.

2. As Paula considers the various time-management tools, what are some of the things she should do?

    ✓ a) Paula should write down the ways that she imagines using the tool to her benefit.

    b) Paula should use all of the tools and decide after a few weeks which tools to keep using.

    ✓ c) Paula should list any potential drawbacks that she might encounter with a particular tool.

    d) Paula should ask friends and family for their advice on which tools she should use.

3. True or False? The benefit of benchmarking is that Paula can take a shortcut by simply picking the time-management tools that were helpful to someone else.

    ___ True

    ✓ False

Activity 4-6

1. Using the guidelines presented, analyze time-management tools and identify the tools you plan to use.

    Time-management tool analysis will vary for each person.

2. How do you think your personal work style, personality, preferences, and your type of job mesh with time-management tools?

    Answers will vary.

3. Which of the recommended time-management tools have you used in the past? Which time-management tools have you found to best suit your preferences and work style? How have you used them to your advantage? Are there any tools that you've found to be ill-suited to your preferences and work style? In what ways did they prove ineffective for you, and why?

Answers will vary.

4. Which of the time-management tools identified did you choose to work with? How do you think these tools will change your approach to time management? Are there other tools you'd like to incorporate into your strategy?

Answers will vary.

5. Did you choose to reject any time-management tools because they don't match your preferences and style of working? If so, which did you reject? Were there any time-management tools that were new to you? Do you think you might like to try out these tools? Why or why not?

Answers will vary.

Lesson 5

Activity 5-1

1. Which of the following considerations are among those that Frank should keep in mind as he begins to create his action plan?

   ✓ a) Frank should consider his goals.

   ✓ b) Frank should consider his personal strengths.

   c) Frank should consider Karen's energy level.

   d) Frank should consider Karen's work preferences.

2. As Frank creates his action plan, he needs to review the available time-management tools, techniques, and strategies. Which of the following are among those that Frank should consider?

   a) Frank should ask Karen to create an action plan for him.

   b) Instead of creating an action plan, Frank should consider working longer hours.

   ✓ c) Frank should consider benchmarking someone else's good example.

   d) An action plan probably won't help Frank, who needs to concentrate on his job.

3. True or False? A written action plan identifies all of the strategies, tools, and techniques you intend to use, and it summarizes the behavioral changes that you hope other people will make.

   ___ True

   ✓ False

Activity 5-2

1. Using the guidelines presented, create an action plan.

   Action plans will vary for each person.

2. As you review the goals you have identified for yourself, are they realistic? What is your short-term goal? What is your long-term goal? What is your time frame for completion?

   Answers will vary.

3. How did reviewing the goals you set for yourself influence your creation of an action plan? How did your goals dictate your action plan development?

   Answers will vary.

4. How did your review of your personal style, motivators, personal strengths, and preferences influence your creation of your action plan? How did you incorporate these various elements into your plan? Were there other elements of your personal style that you wanted to incorporate into the plan, but you weren't sure how to do it? If so, how did you address those issues?

   Answers will vary.

5. Now that you've summarized the behavioral changes you intend to make, how do you feel about moving forward? Do you think these behavioral changes will be difficult for you to implement on the job? Why or why not? How do you think having a written action plan will help to make it easier to implement behavioral changes?

   Answers will vary.

Activity 5-3

1. Naomi needs to begin evaluating her progress. What is the first question she should ask herself?

   a) Naomi should ask herself why she hasn't yet met all of her goals and priorities.

   b) Naomi should ask herself how she can work more quickly.

   c) Naomi should ask herself who she can appropriately delegate projects to.

   ✓ d) Naomi should ask herself whether she has met her goals.

2. If Naomi decides that she has effectively met her goals and addressed her priorities and her critical and valuable tasks, then what are the next steps she should take?

   ✓ a) Naomi should rate her time-management effectiveness on a scale of 1 to 5.

   b) Naomi should ask others for their advice in moving forward productively.

   ✓ c) Naomi should summarize her results, noting how she has become more productive at work.

   d) Naomi should curtail her efforts at managing her time.

3. True or False? If Naomi has effectively evaluated her time-management work, she will have identified any outstanding issues as well as the strategies she will use to address them.

   ✓ True

   ___ False

SOLUTIONS

1. Using the guidelines presented, evaluate your time-management process.

   Time-management evaluations will vary for each person.

2. As you worked on your action plan, were you pleased with your results? What part of your action plan do you think you will find most helpful, and why?

   Answers will vary.

3. What do you think your stumbling blocks will be as you implement your action plan? Are these stumbling blocks the same issues that you have struggled with in the past?

   Answers will vary.

4. Do you think it will be difficult for you to implement new or different time-management strategies into your routine? Why or why not? Do you think that any of your outstanding time-management problems are intractable? If so, how do you intend to move forward effectively?

   Answers will vary.

GLOSSARY

80/20 rule
A theory that suggests that in any enterprise, 80 percent of the effort expended is nonessential, and 20 percent is essential.

action plan
Your written blueprint, it documents your plans for implementing effective time-management techniques.

benchmark
A standard basis for comparison or evaluation.

burnout
The exhaustion and energy depletion caused by working too hard and too long.

causes
The underlying reasons for your outstanding time-management problems.

criteria
The basic standards for evaluation.

critical task
A task that must be completed.

delegation
The act of empowering someone else to act on your behalf.

diplomatic solutions
Polite, mutually beneficial resolutions to time-related conflicts.

dream
A personal, hopeful vision for your future.

energy allocation
The distribution of a person's energy across activities.

external time wasters
The factors that both waste your time and are created by other people or are beyond your control.

goal
An achievement or accomplishment that you are determined to reach in the future.

internal time wasters
The factors that both waste your time and are self-created or within your control.

issues
Time-management problems that remain unresolved or need further work.

momentum
The strength and energy gathered from productive events.

motivators
The factors that provide people with the incentive and drive to act.

perception
An individual's mental concept.

personal energy sources
The factors that refresh, revitalize, and motivate you.

personal world view
One individual's unique perspective and philosophy about the world and his or her position in it; it may be influenced by the person's education, upbringing, belief system, and values.

priorities
The tasks that you define as critical and valuable.

GLOSSARY

priority alignment
The act of making sure that your time and energy expenditures correlate to the tasks, projects, and activities that you've identified as most important.

reality
The totality of real things and events; an objective assessment of your effort and your activities for a given period of time.

regret
The disappointment experienced due to missed opportunities or unfulfilled potential.

requirements
That which is essential or necessary to complete a task or fulfill an obligation.

strengths
The positive qualities, attributes, and inherent assets that make you uniquely effective.

success
The attainment of a desired outcome.

time analysis
The act of making judgments about your current use of time.

time estimation
The process of forecasting how much time a given activity will take.

time log
A written summary kept for a given period of time that details the activities completed during that time.

time management
The process of strategically managing time.

valuable task
A task that contributes to furthering your goals.

work style
A person's preferred way of working; it includes preferences for noise level, activity level and pace, physical environment, level of interaction with other people, and level of responsibility.

INDEX

INDEX

Effective Time Management